middle
eastern

THE AUSTRALIAN
Women's Weekly

contents

To sample some of the foods of the vast area we label the Middle East, take some of the essential ingredients and choose your favourite: dark purple aubergines, glossy green or black olives, the spices and herbs – cinnamon, cardamom and coriander – the freshness of cut cucumber and to finish off, something delightfully sticky with honey and almonds. Here we offer you a cross section of some of the glorious tastes and textures that so characterise these lands.

Food Director

Pamela Clark

starters and snacks

Dukkah is delicious with olive oil and bread, sprinkled over salads, vegetables, barbecued meat and seafood and soups.

dukkah

⅔ cup (110g) blanched almonds
⅔ cup (110g) hazelnuts
½ cup (75g) sesame seeds
¼ cup (20g) coriander seeds
2 tablespoons cumin seeds
2 teaspoons freshly ground black pepper
2 teaspoons flaked sea salt

1 Preheat oven to 180°C/160°C fan-assisted.
2 Spread almonds and hazelnuts on oven trays, roast in oven about 10 minutes or until toasted. Transfer hazelnuts to a clean tea towel and rub nuts in tea towel to remove as much of the hazelnut skin as possible; cool.
3 Meanwhile, toast sesame seeds in a medium dry frying pan over low heat, stirring occasionally until golden brown. Transfer sesame seeds to a large heatproof bowl; cool.
4 Process almonds and hazelnuts, until chopped finely; add to sesame seeds.
5 Combine coriander and cumin seeds in same medium dry frying pan, cook over low heat, stirring occasionally until fragrant; cool. Grind seeds using a mortar and pestle or spice grinder.
6 Add seeds to almond mixture with pepper and salt; mix well. Store in airtight jars.

makes about 2½ cups
tip Store dukkah in an airtight container for up to one month.

dips

tahini dip

12 cloves garlic
2 teaspoons ground cumin
1 teaspoon grated lemon rind
⅔ cup (160ml) tahini
½ cup (125ml) lemon juice
½ cup (125ml) water

1 Place unpeeled garlic cloves on oven tray, bake, uncovered, in hot oven about 10 minutes or until garlic is soft; cool. Remove skin from cloves.
2 Blend or process garlic, cumin, rind and tahini until combined.
3 Add combined juice and water gradually in a thin stream while motor is operating, process until combined. Spoon into serving bowl, sprinkle with a little extra ground cumin, if desired.

makes *about 1½ cups (375ml)*

aubergine dip

2 large aubergines (1kg)
¼ cup (60ml) plain yogurt
2 tablespoons lemon juice
1 clove garlic, crushed
¼ cup (60ml) tahini
2 teaspoons ground cumin
⅓ cup fresh coriander leaves

1 Pierce aubergines in several places with a skewer. Place whole aubergines on oven tray. Bake, uncovered, in hot oven about 1 hour or until soft; cool 15 minutes.
2 Peel aubergines, chop flesh roughly; discard the skins.
3 Blend or process aubergine flesh with yogurt, juice, garlic, tahini, cumin and coriander until combined. Sprinkle with chopped parsley, if desired.

makes *about 2¼ cups (560ml)*

Serve these dips with a selection of raw vegetable sticks, toasted pitta bread or spicy lavash — thin, flat sheets of unleavened bread available in some supermarkets and delicatessens.

broad bean dip

⅓ cup (80ml) olive oil
1 medium onion (150g), finely chopped
1 clove garlic, crushed
1 teaspoon ground cumin
pinch cayenne pepper
500g frozen broad beans, thawed, peeled
¾ cup (180ml) water
1 tablespoon lemon juice
1 tablespoon chopped fresh dill

1 Heat 1 tablespoon of the oil in pan, add onion, garlic, cumin and pepper, cook, stirring, until onion is soft. Add beans, cook, stirring, 5 minutes.
2 Blend or process bean mixture, remaining oil, water and lemon juice until well combined.
3 Return bean mixture to same pan, stir over heat until heated through; stir in dill. Sprinkle warm dip with a little extra cayenne pepper, if desired.

makes *about 2 cups (500ml)*

hummus

2 teaspoons olive oil
1 medium onion (150g), chopped
2 cloves garlic, crushed
1½ teaspoons ground cumin
2 x 425g cans chickpeas, rinsed, drained
½ cup (125ml) tahini
½ cup (125ml) lemon juice
1 tablespoon fresh coriander leaves
1 teaspoon ground hot paprika
¾ cup (180ml) buttermilk

spicy lavash
480g packet lavash bread
2 tablespoons cajun seasoning

1 Heat oil in pan, add onion and garlic, cook, stirring, until onion is soft. Add cumin, cook, stirring, until fragrant; cool 5 minutes.
2 Blend or process onion mixture, chickpeas, tahini, juice, coriander, paprika and buttermilk until smooth. Spoon into serving bowl, drizzle with a little extra olive oil, if desired. Serve with spicy lavash.

spicy lavash Cut each lavash into 16 triangles, place in single layer on oven trays; sprinkle with seasoning. Toast in hot oven about 5 minutes or until crisp.

makes *about 1 litre (4 cups)*

butterbean dip with pitta crisps

1 clove garlic, crushed
¼ cup fresh flat-leaf parsley leaves
400g can butterbeans, rinsed, drained
1 teaspoon ground cumin
⅓ cup (80ml) olive oil
6 pitta breads, cut into sixths

1 Preheat oven to 200°C/180°C fan-assisted.
2 Blend or process garlic, parsley, beans and cumin until combined. With motor operating, add the oil in a thin, steady stream until mixture is smooth.
3 Place pitta pieces on lightly oiled oven trays; bake about 8 minutes or until browned lightly.
4 Serve dip with pitta crisps.

serves 8
tips This recipe can be made a day ahead. Store pitta crisps in an airtight container.

spinach, leek and cheese pastries

1kg spinach, chopped
2 tablespoons water
2 tablespoons olive oil
1 large leek (500g), chopped
4 cloves garlic, crushed
½ teaspoon ground cumin
½ teaspoon ground cinnamon
¼ cup chopped fresh dill
½ cup chopped fresh parsley
½ cup (80g) pine nuts, toasted
500g feta cheese, crumbled
2 eggs, lightly beaten
12 sheets filo pastry
100g butter, melted

1 Combine spinach and water in large pan, simmer, covered, few minutes or until spinach is wilted, drain; squeeze out excess liquid.
2 Heat oil in pan, add leek, garlic and spices, cook, stirring, until leek is soft and liquid evaporated. Transfer mixture to large bowl, add spinach, herbs, nuts, cheese and eggs; mix well.
3 To prevent pastry drying out, cover with baking parchment then a damp tea towel until you are ready to use it. Layer two sheets of pastry together, brushing each with a little of the butter. Cut layers in half lengthways. Place ⅓ cup spinach mixture at one end of each strip.
4 Fold one corner end of pastry diagonally across filling to other edge to form a triangle. Continue folding to end of strip, retaining triangular shape. Brush triangle with a little more butter. Repeat with remaining pastry, filling and butter. Place triangles on greased oven trays. Bake in moderately hot oven about 15 minutes or until browned.

makes 12

meze

8 large pitta
200g marinated black and green Greek olives

1 Heat or toast the pitta on both sides.
2 Serve the cucumber and yogurt dip, roasted pepper with fried walnuts, baked chilli and oregano feta and fried calamari (see recipes below) with pitta bread and olives.

serves 6

cucumber and yogurt dip

250g plain Greek yogurt
½ (130g) cucumber, deseeded, chopped finely
1 tablespoon finely chopped fresh mint
1 clove garlic, crushed
salt

1 Place the yogurt in a muslin-lined sieve over a bowl; cover and refrigerate for 3 to 4 hours or until thick.
2 Combine drained yogurt with cucumber, mint, garlic and salt to taste in a small bowl.

baked chilli and oregano feta

2 x 200g pieces feta cheese
2 teaspoons extra virgin olive oil
¼ teaspoon chilli flakes
½ teaspoon dried oregano

1 Preheat oven to moderately hot (200°C/180°C fan-assisted).
2 Place both pieces of cheese on separate squares of foil large enough to enclose them. Drizzle cheese with oil; sprinkle with chilli and oregano. Enclose foil to form a parcel.
3 Bake for 10 minutes or until heated through.

roasted pepper with fried walnuts

2 medium (400g) red peppers
2 tablespoons extra virgin olive oil
⅓ cup (35g) whole walnuts
salt and freshly ground black pepper

1 Halve peppers; discard seeds and membranes. Roast under grill or in very hot oven, skin-side up, until skin blisters and blackens. Cover pepper pieces with plastic or paper for 5 minutes; peel away skin, then slice flesh thickly.
2 Combine oil, walnuts, salt and pepper in small saucepan; stir gently over low heat until warm and walnuts are crisp.
3 Serve pepper slices drizzled with warmed walnuts and oil.

fried calamari

800g small whole calamari (squid)
olive oil, for deep-frying
plain flour
salt
lemon wedges, for serving

1 Gently separate the body and tentacles of the calamari by pulling on the tentacles. Cut the head from the tentacles just below the eyes and discard the head. Trim the long tentacle from each calamari. Remove the clear quill from inside the body. Peel the side flaps from the body with salted fingers, then peel away the dark skin (the salt gives more grip). Cut the body into 2cm rings.
2 Wash the calamari well and pat dry with absorbent paper. Heat the oil in a large pan. Toss the calamari in flour seasoned with salt; shake away the excess.
3 Deep-fry the calamari, in batches, until just browned and tender; drain on absorbent paper. Serve calamari with lemon wedges.

Meze are 'little bits' or appetisers. You can start the meal with this platter and, except for the calamari, it can be left on the table throughout the meal to accompany the main course.

minted beef and pine nut triangles

2 teaspoons olive oil
1 small onion (80g), chopped
2 cloves garlic, crushed
1 teaspoon ground cumin
1 teaspoon ground coriander
300g minced beef
2 tablespoons chopped fresh mint
2 tablespoons pine nuts
2 medium potatoes (400g), chopped
½ cup (60g) grated cheddar cheese
10 sheets filo pastry
125g butter, melted

tomato sauce
2 teaspoons olive oil
1 small onion (80g), chopped
2 cloves garlic, crushed
425g can crushed tomatoes
1 tablespoon tomato paste
2 teaspoons brown sugar
2 tablespoons chopped fresh mint

1 Heat oil in pan, add onion, garlic and spices, cook, stirring, until onion is soft. Add beef, mint and nuts, cook, stirring, until beef is browned.
2 Cook potatoes until soft. Mash until smooth, add cheese. Combine with beef mixture and mix well.
3 To prevent pastry drying out, cover with baking parchment then a damp tea towel. Layer two sheets of pastry together, brushing each with butter. Cut layers into three strips lengthways. Place a rounded tablespoon of mixture at one end of each strip.
4 Fold one corner end of pastry diagonally across filling to other edge to form a triangle. Continue folding to end of strip, retaining triangular shape. Make rest of pastries in same way. Place pastries on greased oven trays, brush with more butter. Bake in moderately hot oven about 8 minutes or until browned. Serve with tomato sauce.

tomato sauce Heat oil in pan, add onion and garlic, cook, stirring, until onion is soft. Add undrained crushed tomatoes, paste, sugar and mint, simmer, uncovered, about 5 minutes or until slightly thickened.

makes *15*

cheese crescent pastries

80g butter, melted
⅓ cup (80ml) olive oil
¼ cup (60ml) water
2 cups (300g) plain flour
1 egg, lightly beaten

filling
1 cup (200g) grated firm feta cheese
2 hard-boiled eggs, chopped
2 tablespoons finely chopped fresh
    parsley
40g packaged cream cheese

1 Combine butter, oil and water in bowl. Add sifted flour, 1 tablespoon at a time, stirring to a smooth paste between additions. Continue adding flour until a soft dough is formed. Turn onto lightly floured surface, knead gently until smooth. Cover, refrigerate 1 hour.
2 Divide pastry in half, roll each half between sheets of lightly floured baking parchment until as thin as possible. Cover, refrigerate 30 minutes. Cut 8cm rounds from pastry, re-roll pastry scraps. Refrigerate pastry between rolling if it becomes too soft to handle.
3 Drop rounded teaspoons of filling into centre of each round. Fold over and pinch edges to seal. Place on greased oven trays, brush with egg. Bake in moderately hot oven about 15 minutes until lightly browned.

filling Combine all ingredients in bowl; mix well.

makes *about 45*

Although feta is commonly associated with Greek cooking, it is the most popular cheese eaten in the Middle East.

olive oil pastries with cheeses and mint

2½ cups (375g) plain flour
1 egg
½ cup (125ml) water, approximately
⅓ cup (80ml) olive oil
1 teaspoon salt
extra olive oil, for shallow-frying

filling
1 cup (200g) finely crumbled feta cheese
1 cup (100g) grated hard goats' milk cheese
2 teaspoons finely chopped fresh mint leaves
2 teaspoons finely chopped fresh dill
2 eggs, beaten lightly
freshly ground black pepper

1 In a food processor, combine flour, egg, water, oil and salt; process until ingredients just come together. Turn onto a board, knead gently until smooth. Cover pastry in cling film, refrigerate for 30 minutes.
2 Divide pastry into 4 even pieces. Roll one piece until 2mm thick. Cut out as many 8cm rounds as possible. Reserve scraps. Repeat with remaining 3 pieces.
3 Knead scraps lightly and re-roll; cut out rounds to make 30 rounds in total.
4 Place 2 teaspoons of filling in the centre of each pastry round; brush edges with water. Fold pastry over to form semi-circles; press edges together with a fork to seal.
5 Shallow-fry pastries, in batches, in olive oil until browned on both sides; drain on kitchen paper.
6 Serve sprinkled with extra mint leaves, if desired.

filling Combine all ingredients in a medium bowl.

makes about 30
tips Pastries can be prepared several hours ahead. Fry pastries just before serving.

potato cakes with pepper tabbouleh

2 large potatoes (600g), peeled, grated
3 spring onions, finely chopped
1 egg yolk
¼ cup (30g) soya flour
1 teaspoon ground coriander
vegetable oil for shallow-frying

pepper tabbouleh
1 medium yellow pepper (200g)
1 medium red pepper (200g)
⅓ cup (55g) bulgar wheat
1½ cups finely chopped fresh parsley
⅓ cup (80ml) olive oil
¼ cup (60ml) lemon juice

dressing
1 cup (250ml) plain yogurt
2 teaspoons ground cumin
¾ teaspoon ground turmeric
1 teaspoon sugar

1 Place potatoes between several sheets of kitchen paper, press paper to remove as much moisture as possible. Combine potatoes, onions, egg yolk, flour and coriander in bowl; mix well.
2 Heat oil in pan, add ⅓ cup potato mixture in batches; flatten to 10cm rounds. Cook cakes slowly until browned, turn, brown other side; drain on kitchen paper, keep warm. Serve topped with pepper tabbouleh; drizzle with dressing.

pepper tabbouleh Quarter peppers, remove seeds and membranes. Grill peppers, skin side up, until skin blisters and blackens; peel away skin, chop flesh finely. Place bulgar wheat in small heatproof bowl, cover with boiling water, stand 20 minutes, drain. Place bulgar between several sheets of kitchen paper, press paper to remove as much moisture as possible. Transfer bulgar to bowl, add pepper, parsley, oil and juice; mix well.

dressing Combine all ingredients in bowl; mix well.

serves 6

mushroom and spinach cigars

2 tablespoons olive oil
2 small red onions (200g), finely chopped
2 cloves garlic, crushed
1 teaspoon ground cinnamon
½ teaspoon ground allspice
½ teaspoon ground coriander
2 large flat mushrooms (250g), finely chopped
250g spinach, finely shredded
2 teaspoons lemon juice
6 sheets filo pastry
50g butter, melted

1 Heat oil in pan, add onions, garlic and spices, cook, stirring, until fragrant. Add mushrooms, cook, stirring, 5 minutes or until liquid has evaporated.
2 Stir in spinach and juice, cook, stirring, about 3 minutes or until spinach is wilted and any liquid has evaporated; cool to room temperature.
3 To prevent pastry drying out, cover with baking parchment then a damp tea towel. Layer three sheets of pastry together, brushing each with a little butter. Cut layers into eight squares. Place 1 tablespoon of mushroom mixture along one end of each square. Roll pastry over filling, fold in sides, roll up. Make remaining cigars in the same way.
4 Place cigars about 2cm apart on greased oven tray, brush with more butter. Bake in hot oven about 10 minutes or until browned.

makes 16

spicy lamb pizzas

1 teaspoon dried yeast
½ teaspoon sugar
⅔ cup (160ml) warm water
1½ cups (225g) plain flour
½ teaspoon salt
¼ cup (60ml) olive oil
2 tablespoons pine nuts, toasted
1 tablespoon chopped fresh coriander
   leaves

lamb topping
2 teaspoons olive oil
250g minced lamb
1 small onion (80g), finely chopped
1 clove garlic, crushed
½ teaspoon ground cinnamon
1 teaspoon ground cumin
½ teaspoon sambal oelek
1 small courgette (90g), grated
2 tablespoons tomato paste
1 large tomato (250g), finely chopped

1 Combine yeast, sugar and ¼ cup (60ml) of the water in small bowl, cover, stand in warm place about 20 minutes or until mixture is frothy.
2 Sift flour and salt into bowl. Stir in remaining water, yeast mixture and oil; mix to a soft dough. Knead dough on floured surface about 5 minutes or until smooth and elastic.
3 Place dough in oiled bowl, cover, stand in warm place about 1 hour or until dough has doubled in size. Turn dough onto lightly floured surface, knead until smooth. Divide dough into 18 pieces, roll each to a 10cm round.
4 Place rounds onto greased oven trays, top each with a tablespoon of lamb topping, leaving a 1cm border. Sprinkle with nuts; brush edges with a little extra oil. Bake in moderately hot oven about 15 minutes or until cooked and browned. Sprinkle with coriander.

lamb topping Heat oil in pan, add lamb, cook, stirring, until browned; remove from pan. Add onion, garlic, spices, sambal oelek and courgette to same pan, cook, stirring, until onion is soft. Return lamb to pan, add paste and tomato, cook, stirring, about 5 minutes or until thickened slightly; cool.

makes 18

These little crispy pizzas will disappear quickly!
Unlike their traditional Italian relatives, they contain
no cheese.

lamb and pine nut boats

2 teaspoons olive oil
1 small onion (80g), chopped finely
2 cloves garlic, crushed
2 teaspoons ground cumin
400g minced lamb
1 medium tomato (150g), chopped finely
1 tablespoon finely chopped fresh flat-leaf parsley
1 tablespoon lemon juice
2 tablespoons sumac
3 sheets ready-rolled shortcrust pastry
1 egg, beaten lightly
2 tablespoons pine nuts
1 tablespoon finely chopped fresh flat-leaf parsley, extra
½ cup (140g) plain yogurt

1 Heat oil in small frying pan; cook onion, garlic and cumin, stirring, until onion softens. Place onion mixture in medium bowl with minced lamb, tomato, parsley, juice and half the sumac; mix until combined.
2 Preheat oven to 200°C/180°C fan-assisted. Oil two oven trays.
3 Cut each pastry sheet into nine squares. Brush two opposing sides of pastry square with beaten egg; place 1 level tablespoon of filling along centre of square. Bring egg-brushed sides together then push the two unbrushed sides inward to widen centre opening, making boat shape and showing filling. Sprinkle some of the nuts on exposed filling; place boat on tray. Repeat process, spacing boats 4cm apart on oven trays.
4 Bake, uncovered, about 20 minutes or until browned lightly and cooked through. Sprinkle with parsley.
5 Serve combined yogurt and remaining sumac in small bowl with boats.

makes 27

spicy prawns

18 uncooked medium king prawns (720g)
2 cloves garlic, crushed
1 fresh long red chilli, chopped finely
2 tablespoons olive oil
1 tablespoon lemon juice

1 Shell and devein prawns, leaving tails intact. Combine garlic, chilli and oil in medium bowl, add prawns; toss prawns to coat in marinade. Cover; refrigerate 3 hours or overnight.
2 Cook prawns in large heated frying pan, in batches, until just changed in colour. Serve prawns drizzled with juice.

makes 18

stuffed vine leaves

½ cup (125ml) extra virgin olive oil
1 bunch (400g) spring onions, chopped
½ cup (80g) pine nuts
2 cloves garlic, crushed
1¼ cups (250g) white medium-grain
  rice
½ cup finely chopped fresh flat-leaf
  parsley
⅓ cup finely chopped fresh dill
½ cup (80g) sultanas
¼ cup (60ml) lemon juice
200g packet vine leaves in brine
1 (140g) lemon, sliced thinly
3 cups (750ml) water

1 Heat half the oil in a large frying pan; cook onion, pine nuts and garlic, stirring, until onion is softened and pine nuts are browned lightly. Add rice; cook, stirring, for 1 minute. Add herbs, sultanas, juice and remaining oil; remove from heat.

2 Rinse vine leaves under cold water; drain well and pat dry. Line base of a large heavy-based saucepan with about 10 of the damaged vine leaves. Place another leaf, vein-side-up, on a board. Cut off stem if it's attached. Place 1 level tablespoon of rice mixture in the centre of the leaf, above the point where the stem was. Fold in two sides; roll tightly to enclose filling. Repeat with remaining leaves and rice mixture.

3 Place rolls, in a single layer, on leaves in the pan; pack in tightly so they cannot unroll during cooking. Cover rolls with lemon slices, then remaining vine leaves. Place a large heatproof plate on top of rolls so they can't move during cooking. Add the water to the saucepan; bring to the boil. Reduce heat; simmer gently, covered, for about 1 hour or until the rice is cooked.

4 Serve stuffed vine leaves at room temperature.

makes *about 32*

Stuffed vine leaves can be served as part of a platter of mezethes, as finger food or a tasty snack.

spiced lamb vine leaf parcels

25 (120g) packaged vine leaves in brine
2 large tomatoes (500g), sliced
1 cup (250ml) tomato purée
2 tablespoons olive oil
2 tablespoons lemon juice
1 cup (250ml) chicken stock

filling
1½ tablespoons olive oil
½ small onion (40g), chopped
1 clove garlic, crushed
2 tablespoons white short-grain rice
1 tablespoon raisins, chopped
½ cup (125ml) water
1 teaspoon ground cinnamon
1 teaspoon ground coriander
2 tablespoons chopped fresh coriander
1½ tablespoons flaked almonds,
    toasted, chopped
150g minced lamb

1 Place vine leaves in bowl, cover with cold water, stand 5 minutes; drain. Rinse leaves under cold water; drain well. Place leaves vein side up on board, place a rounded teaspoon of filling on each leaf, roll up firmly, folding in sides to enclose filling.
2 Cover base of 25cm heavy-based pan with tomato slices. Place rolls in single layer over tomatoes, pour over combined tomato puree, oil, juice and stock. Place a plate on top of rolls to keep rolls in position during cooking. Simmer, covered, over low heat about 1 hour or until cooked through.

filling Heat oil in pan, add onion and garlic, cook, stirring, until onion is soft. Add rice and raisins, mix well. Add water and spices, simmer, uncovered, about 5 minutes or until liquid is absorbed; cool. Stir in remaining ingredients.

makes 25

felafel

1 tablespoon olive oil
1 medium onion (150g), roughly
    chopped
1 clove garlic, crushed
2 medium potatoes (400g), chopped
1¼ cups (185g) frozen broad beans,
    thawed, peeled
½ teaspoon ground cinnamon
½ teaspoon ground cumin
¼ teaspoon chilli powder
⅓ cup fresh parsley leaves
plain flour
vegetable oil for deep-frying

yogurt dip
1 small cucumber (130g)
¾ cup (180ml) plain yogurt
½ teaspoon ground cumin
2 teaspoons chopped fresh mint

1 Heat olive oil in pan, add onion and garlic, cook, stirring, until onion is soft. Boil, steam or microwave potatoes until soft; drain, mash until smooth.
2 Process onion mixture, potatoes, beans, spices and parsley until smooth.
3 Drop rounded teaspoons of mixture onto baking parchment-covered trays, refrigerate 1 hour. Toss felafel in flour, roll into balls; flatten slightly. Deep-fry felafel in hot vegetable oil in batches until lightly browned; drain on absorbent paper. Serve with yogurt dip.

yogurt dip Cut cucumber in half lengthways; remove seeds, finely chop cucumber. Combine cucumber with remaining ingredients in bowl; mix well.

makes about 30

chickpea, lentil and bean soup

1 tablespoon olive oil
1 large red onion (300g), chopped
2 cloves garlic, crushed
1 teaspoon ground cumin
1 teaspoon ground turmeric
1 teaspoon ground sweet paprika
½ teaspoon ground cinnamon
2 x 425g cans chickpeas, rinsed,
    drained
340g can red kidney beans, rinsed,
    drained
½ cup (100g) red lentils
1.25 litres (5 cups) vegetable stock
¼ cup (60ml) lemon juice
⅓ cup chopped fresh mint
500g spinach, shredded

1 Heat oil in pan, add onion, garlic and spices, cook, stirring, until onion is soft.
2 Stir in peas, beans, lentils, stock, juice and mint, simmer, covered, about 20 minutes, stirring occasionally, or until lentils are tender.
3 Stir in spinach, simmer, uncovered, about 5 minutes or until spinach is just wilted.

serves 6

tomato, lentil and coriander soup

1 tablespoon olive oil
2 medium onions (300g), chopped
3 cloves garlic, crushed
½ teaspoon garam masala
½ teaspoon sambal oelek
¼ cup (60ml) tomato paste
12 medium tomatoes (1.5kg), peeled,
    deseeded, chopped
1.5 litre (6 cups) vegetable stock
½ cup (100g) red lentils
2 teaspoons sugar
⅓ cup chopped fresh coriander leaves

coriander yogurt
1 cup (250ml) plain yogurt
2 tablespoons chopped fresh parsley
2 tablespoons chopped fresh coriander
    leaves
1 teaspoon ground coriander

1 Heat oil in large pan, add onions, garlic, garam masala and sambal oelek, cook over medium heat, stirring, until onions are soft.
2 Add paste, tomatoes, stock, lentils, sugar and coriander, simmer, stirring, uncovered, about 20 minutes or until lentils are tender. Serve topped with coriander yogurt.

coriander yogurt Combine all ingredients in small bowl; mix well.

serves 6

main courses

chicken with couscous stuffing and green olive salsa

1.6kg chicken
20g butter, melted
20 baby vine tomatoes (400g)
1 tablespoon olive oil

couscous stuffing
1 teaspoon olive oil
1 medium onion (150g), chopped finely
1½ cups (375ml) chicken stock
¼ cup (60ml) olive oil, extra
1 tablespoon finely grated lemon rind
¼ cup (60ml) lemon juice
1 cup (200g) couscous
½ cup (70g) roasted slivered almonds
1 cup (140g) stoned dried dates,
   chopped finely
1 teaspoon ground cinnamon
1 teaspoon smoked paprika
1 egg, beaten lightly

green olive salsa
1½ cups (180g) pitted green olives,
   chopped coarsely
⅓ cup (80ml) olive oil
1 tablespoon cider vinegar
1 shallot (25g), chopped finely
1 fresh long red chilli, chopped finely
¼ cup coarsely chopped fresh flat-leaf parsley
¼ cup coarsely chopped fresh mint

1 Make couscous stuffing.
2 Preheat oven to 200°C/180°C fan-assisted.
3 Wash chicken under cold water; pat dry inside and out with absorbent paper. Fill large cavity loosely with couscous stuffing; tie legs together with kitchen string.
4 Half fill large baking dish with water; place chicken on oiled wire rack over dish. Brush chicken all over with butter; roast, uncovered, 15 minutes. Reduce oven temperature to 180°C/160°C fan-assisted; roast, uncovered, about 1½ hours or until cooked through. Remove chicken from rack; cover, stand 20 minutes.
5 Meanwhile, place tomatoes on oven tray; drizzle with oil. Roast, uncovered, about 20 minutes or until soft and lightly browned.
6 Combine ingredients for green olive salsa in small bowl.
7 Serve chicken with tomatoes and salsa.

couscous stuffing Heat oil in small frying pan; cook onion, stirring, until onion is soft. Combine stock, extra oil, rind and juice in medium saucepan; bring to a boil. Remove from heat. Add couscous, cover; stand about 5 minutes or until liquid is absorbed, fluffing with fork occasionally. Stir in onion, nuts, dates, spices and egg.

Salsa is a spicy sauce of chopped, usually uncooked, vegetables or fruit. The olives and mint in this version give it a real Middle-Eastern flavour.

Because of their acidic nature, pomegranates should only be cooked in stainless steel or enamel pans to prevent discolouration.

duck in pomegranate sauce

2 small ducks (1.75kg each)
1 medium pomegranate (320g)
1 cup (250ml) water
1 tablespoon olive oil
1 medium onion (150g), sliced
2 cloves garlic, crushed
1 teaspoon ground turmeric
1 teaspoon ground cinnamon
1 teaspoon ground cumin
1 teaspoon ground coriander
1 cup (250ml) chicken stock
1 tablespoon lemon juice
¼ cup (50g) brown sugar
2 tablespoons ground almonds

1 Place ducks on wire rack over large baking dish. Bake, uncovered, in moderately hot oven about 1 hour or until browned and just cooked. Remove from oven, cover; stand 30 minutes.

2 Cut pomegranate in half; scoop out seeds, reserve ¼ cup (60ml) of the seeds. Combine remaining seeds and water in stainless steel or enamel pan, bring to boil; strain.

3 Heat oil in stainless steel or enamel pan, add onion, garlic and spices, cook, stirring, until onion is soft. Add pomegranate liquid, stock, juice, sugar and almonds, cook, stirring, over heat until mixture boils and thickens slightly.

4 Place duck on board, cut through breastbone, using poultry shears. Cut on either side of backbone; remove backbone.

5 Remove breastbone and ribcage from each half of duck. Cut each half into two pieces. Repeat with remaining duck. Grill duck, skin side up, until skin is crisp. Place duck pieces on serving plate, pour over sauce, top with reserved pomegranate seeds then chopped pistachios and coriander leaves, if desired.

serves *4 to 6*

paprika chicken with raisin & coriander pilaf

8 skinless chicken thighs (1.3kg)
2 tablespoons lemon juice
3 cloves garlic, crushed
½ teaspoon hot paprika
1 teaspoon sweet paprika
1 teaspoon ground cinnamon
¾ cup (200g) plain yogurt
1 tablespoon olive oil
1 medium onion (150g), chopped finely
2 cups (200g) basmati rice
1 litre (4 cups) chicken stock
½ cup (85g) chopped raisins
¾ cup chopped fresh coriander

1 Combine chicken, juice, garlic and spices in large bowl, cover; refrigerate 3 hours or overnight.
2 Cook chicken, in batches, on heated oiled grill plate or barbecue, brushing with a little of the yogurt, until browned and cooked through.
3 Meanwhile, heat oil in medium saucepan; cook onion, stirring, until softened. Add rice; stir to coat in onion mixture. Add stock; bring to a boil. Reduce heat; simmer, covered, stirring occasionally, about 25 minutes or until rice is almost tender. Stir in raisins; cook, covered, 5 minutes.
4 Stir coriander into pilaf off the heat just before serving. Top pilaf with chicken and remaining yogurt.

serves 4

chicken in date sauce with almonds and orange couscous

1 tablespoon olive oil
1 large onion (200g), sliced thinly
1½ teaspoons ground cinnamon
2 teaspoons finely grated orange rind
¼ teaspoon cayenne pepper
1½ cups (375ml) chicken stock
½ cup (70g) pitted dates, chopped
   coarsely
1 large barbecued chicken (900g),
   quartered
1 cup (250ml) orange juice
1 cup (250ml) water
2 cups (400g) couscous
20g butter
¼ cup (35g) roasted slivered almonds

1 Heat oil in large frying pan; cook onion, stirring, until browned lightly. Add cinnamon, rind, cayenne and stock; bring to a boil. Simmer, uncovered, 4 minutes. Add dates and chicken; stir until mixture is heated through.
2 Meanwhile, combine orange juice and the water in large saucepan; bring to a boil. Remove from heat; add couscous. Cover; stand about 5 minutes or until liquid is absorbed, fluffing with fork occasionally. Stir in butter.
3 Serve chicken mixture sprinkled with almonds on bed of couscous.

serves 4

roast turkey breast with couscous stuffing

½ cup (80g) sultanas
½ cup (125ml) lemon juice
4.5kg butterflied turkey breast joint
1 cup (250ml) chicken stock
¼ cup (60ml) olive oil
1 cup (200g) couscous
¼ cup (40g) toasted pepitas
¼ cup (35g) toasted slivered almonds
¼ cup (35g) toasted pecans, chopped
   coarsely
¼ cup cup coarsely chopped fresh
   flat-leaf parsley
¼ cup cup coarsely chopped fresh
   coriander
2 eggs, beaten lightly
1½ cups (375ml) water
⅓ cup (50g) plain flour
2 cups (500ml) chicken stock, extra
3 cups (750ml) water, extra

paprika rub
1 teaspoon fennel seeds
1 teaspoon sweet paprika
½ teaspoon ground ginger
2 teaspoons salt
2 cloves garlic, quartered
2 tablespoons olive oil

1 Soak sultanas in small bowl in half of the lemon juice. Make paprika rub.
2 Preheat oven to moderate.
3 Place turkey flat on board, skin-side down; cover with cling film. Using rolling pin or meat mallet, flatten turkey meat to an even thickness all over.
4 Combine stock, oil and remaining lemon juice in medium saucepan; bring to a boil. Remove from heat; stir in couscous. Cover; stand about 5 minutes or until liquid is absorbed, fluffing with fork occasionally. Transfer couscous mixture to large bowl; stir in sultana mixture, pepitas, nuts, herbs and egg.
5 With pointed end of turkey breast facing away from you, place stuffing horizontally along centre of turkey. Bring the pointed end of breast over stuffing, securing to the neck skin flap with toothpicks. Working from the centre out, continue securing sides of turkey together with toothpicks (you will have a rectangular roll of turkey in front of you). Tie securely with kitchen string at 4cm intervals.
6 Place turkey roll on oiled wire rack in large shallow flameproof baking dish; add the water to the dish. Rub turkey roll with paprika rub; cover dish tightly with two layers of greased foil. Roast in moderate oven 1 hour. Uncover; roast in moderate oven about 45 minutes or until turkey roll is cooked though. Transfer turkey roll to large serving platter; cover to keep warm.
7 Place dish with juice over heat, add flour; cook, stirring, until mixture bubbles and is well browned. Gradually stir in the extra stock and the extra water; bring to a boil. Reduce heat; simmer, stirring, until gravy boils and thickens. Strain gravy into large jug; serve with turkey.

paprika rub Using mortar and pestle, crush ingredients until smooth.

serves between 8 and 12, depending on menu
tip Order a 4.5kg fresh boned and butterflied turkey breast from your butcher for this recipe.

This recipe provides an interesting twist to the traditional Christmas turkey dinner.

coriander and chilli grilled chicken fillets

6 chicken thigh fillets (660g), halved

coriander chilli sauce
8 spring onions, chopped coarsely
3 cloves garlic, quartered
3 fresh small red chillies, chopped
   coarsely
¼ cup loosely packed fresh coriander
   leaves
1 teaspoon white sugar
1 tablespoon fish sauce
¼ cup (60ml) lime juice

chickpea salad
2 x 300g cans chickpeas, rinsed, drained
2 medium plum tomatoes (150g),
   chopped coarsely
2 spring onions, chopped finely
2 tablespoons lime juice
1 cup coarsely chopped fresh coriander
1 tablespoon olive oil

1 Make coriander chilli sauce.
2 Cook chicken, in batches, on heated oiled grill plate (or grill or barbecue) until almost cooked through. Brush about two-thirds of the coriander chilli sauce all over chicken; cook further 5 minutes or until chicken is cooked through.
3 Meanwhile, combine ingredients for chickpea salad in large bowl; toss gently.
4 Serve chickpea salad with chicken; sprinkle with remaining coriander chilli sauce.

coriander chilli sauce Blend or process onions, garlic, chilli, coriander and sugar until finely chopped. Add sauce and juice; blend until well combined.

serves 4

chicken, cinnamon and prune stew

2 tablespoons olive oil
2kg chicken thigh fillets
3 teaspoons cumin seeds
3 teaspoons ground coriander
1 tablespoon smoked paprika
3 teaspoons ground cumin
4 cinnamon sticks
4 medium onions (600g), sliced thinly
8 cloves garlic, crushed
1 litre (4 cups) chicken stock
1 cup (170g) pitted prunes
½ cup (80g) roasted blanched almonds
¼ cup coarsely chopped fresh flat-leaf
   parsley

1 Heat half the oil in large saucepan; cook chicken, in batches, until browned.
2 Meanwhile, dry-fry spices in small heated frying pan, stirring, until fragrant.
3 Heat remaining oil in same saucepan; cook onion and garlic, stirring, until onion softens. Return chicken to pan with spices and stock; bring to a boil. Simmer, covered, 40 minutes.
4 Stir in prunes; simmer, uncovered, for about 20 minutes or until chicken is tender. Stir in nuts and parsley.

serves 8

spring roast lamb with mint sauce

2 tablespoons extra virgin olive oil
4 cloves garlic, crushed
2 tablespoons lemon juice
2 tablespoons fresh oregano leaves
salt and freshly ground black pepper
2kg boned leg of lamb
1kg desiree potatoes, cut into wedges
1 cup (250ml) chicken stock
2 sprigs fresh rosemary stems

mint sauce
2 cups firmly packed fresh mint leaves
2 tablespoons ground almonds
2 cloves garlic, quartered
⅓ cup (80ml) extra virgin olive oil
2 tablespoons lemon juice

1 Combine oil, garlic, juice, oregano, salt and pepper in a small bowl. Rub lamb all over with garlic mixture, inside and out. Cover, refrigerate for 3 hours or overnight.
2 Preheat the oven to moderately hot (200°C/180°C fan-assisted).
3 Place the potatoes in the base of a large lightly oiled baking dish. Pour stock over potatoes; top with rosemary sprigs. Place lamb on top of potatoes. Roast, uncovered, for about 1 hour or until lamb is cooked as desired.
4 Remove lamb from the dish; stand, covered, for 15 minutes.
5 Increase oven temperature to very hot (250°C/230°C fan-assisted). Roast potatoes for a further 15 minutes or until browned.
6 Make mint sauce
7 Serve lamb with potatoes and mint sauce.

mint sauce Blend or process mint, almond and garlic until finely chopped. Transfer mixture to a bowl; stir in oil and juice. Season to taste with salt and pepper.

serves 6

marinated lemony lamb kebabs

1kg boneless lamb
1 tablespoon olive oil

marinade
2 large onions (400g), chopped
2 cloves garlic, crushed
½ cup (125ml) olive oil
¼ cup (60ml) lemon juice
1 teaspoon ground cumin
½ teaspoon ground ginger
1 teaspoon ground coriander

tomato sauce
425g can tomatoes
1 small fresh red chilli, finely chopped
½ teaspoon ground cumin
¼ teaspoon ground cinnamon

1 Cut lamb into 3cm cubes. Combine lamb and marinade in bowl, cover; refrigerate several hours or overnight.
2 Thread lamb onto skewers, heat oil in pan, add kebabs in batches, cook until browned all over and cooked through. Serve with couscous if desired, and tomato sauce.

marinade Process all ingredients until well combined.

tomato sauce Combine undrained crushed tomatoes with remaining ingredients in small pan, simmer, uncovered, about 5 minutes or until slightly thickened.

serves *4*
tip *Soak bamboo skewers in water for several hours or overnight to prevent them from burning.*

lamb and chickpea casserole

1kg diced boneless lamb
1 teaspoon ground sweet paprika
1 teaspoon ground cumin
50g ghee
2 large onions (400g), sliced
½ teaspoon ground turmeric
2 x 425g cans tomatoes
2 teaspoons sugar
300g can chickpeas, rinsed, drained
2 teaspoons chopped fresh thyme
1 tablespoon chopped fresh parsley

1 Combine lamb, paprika and cumin in bowl, mix well, cover; refrigerate several hours or overnight.
2 Heat ghee in pan, add lamb mixture and onions, cook, stirring, until onions are soft; stir in turmeric.
3 Add undrained crushed tomatoes and sugar, simmer, covered, about 40 minutes or until lamb is just tender. Add chickpeas and herbs, simmer, uncovered, about 10 minutes or until lamb is tender and sauce thickened slightly.

serves *4 to 6*

Preserved lemons are lemons that have been bottled in salt and lemon juice or oil for several months; their flavour is subtle and perfumed.

lamb cutlets with preserved lemon yoghurt

1 teaspoon cumin seeds
2 teaspoons ground coriander
1 teaspoon ground cinnamon
1 teaspoon ground turmeric
2 tablespoons lemon juice
12 (480g) trimmed lamb cutlets
sea salt flakes and freshly ground
   pepper
1 (40g) preserved lemon wedge, rind
   only, chopped finely
1 tablespoon finely chopped fresh
   parsley

preserved lemon yogurt
1 cup (280g) plain Greek yogurt
2 teaspoons lemon juice
1 (40g) preserved lemon wedge, rind
   only, chopped finely

1 Combine spices and lemon juice in a bowl to form a paste. Rub cutlets with paste; cover and refrigerate for 1 hour.
2 Make preserved lemon yogurt.
3 Cook the lamb cutlets on a heated, oiled barbecue (or grill or grill pan) until browned on both sides and cooked as desired. Season with sea salt flakes and freshly ground pepper.
4 Serve topped with preserved lemon yogurt and sprinkled with combined chopped preserved lemon and parsley.

preserved lemon yogurt Combine yoghurt, juice and lemon in a small bowl.

makes 12
tip Rinse the preserved lemons well, then remove and discard the flesh, using the rind only.

spicy braised lamb and yogurt

1 medium onion (150g), chopped
    coarsely
1 tablespoon grated fresh ginger
2 cloves garlic, crushed
1 teaspoon coriander seeds
1 teaspoon cumin seeds
½ teaspoon cardamom seeds
2 tablespoons lime juice
2.5kg leg of lamb, boned, chopped
    coarsely
30g ghee
¼ teaspoon cayenne pepper
2 teaspoons ground turmeric
1 teaspoon garam masala
⅔ cup (190g) plain yogurt
⅔ cup (160ml) double cream
1 cup (250ml) water
400g can chickpeas, rinsed, drained
2 medium tomatoes (380g), chopped
    coarsely
1 tablespoon plain flour
2 tablespoons water, extra
⅓ cup chopped fresh flat-leaf parsley

1 Blend or process onion, ginger, garlic, seeds and juice until well combined. Place blended mixture and lamb in medium bowl; stir until lamb is well coated. Cover; marinate in refrigerator 3 hours or overnight.
2 Heat ghee in large saucepan; add cayenne pepper, turmeric and garam masala; stir over medium heat 1 minute.
3 Stir in yogurt, then lamb; stir over high heat until lamb is well browned. Stir in combined cream and water; bring to a boil. Reduce heat; simmer, uncovered, about 1 hour or until lamb is tender. Stir in chickpeas and tomato.
4 Stir in blended flour and the extra water; stir over high heat until sauce boils and thickens. Stir in parsley; serve with lime wedges, if desired.

serves 6

tips *Ask your butcher to bone the leg of lamb for you. Recipe can be made a day ahead and refrigerated, covered.*

roast lamb with spiced yogurt crust

2kg leg of lamb
4 cloves garlic, quartered
2 teaspoons ground sweet paprika
2 teaspoons ground cumin
1 teaspoon ground turmeric
1 teaspoon ground coriander
1 teaspoon ground black pepper
½ teaspoon ground cardamom
½ teaspoon saffron threads
2 teaspoons grated lemon rind
2 cups (500ml) plain yogurt

1 Makes 16 x 4cm deep cuts into lamb, press garlic into cuts.
2 Combine ground spices, saffron, rind and yogurt in bowl; mix well. Spread spiced yogurt over lamb, cover; refrigerate overnight.
3 Place lamb on wire rack in baking dish, add enough water to cover base of baking dish. Bake, uncovered, in moderate oven about 1½ hours or until crust is browned and lamb tender. Remove from oven, cover loosely with foil; stand 30 minutes before carving. Serve with char-grilled tomatoes and vegetables, if desired.

serves 6 to 8

lamb with chermoulla

2 tablespoons grated lemon rind
2 cloves garlic, chopped coarsely
2 small fresh red chillies, deseeded,
    chopped coarsely
1 tablespoon grated fresh ginger
¼ cup chopped fresh flat-leaf parsley
¼ cup chopped fresh coriander
1 teaspoon sweet paprika
¼ cup (60ml) olive oil
8 lamb forequarter chops (1.5kg)

1 Blend or process lemon rind, garlic, chilli, ginger, herbs, paprika and oil until well combined. Place lamb in single layer in shallow dish; coat lamb in chermoulla paste. Cover; refrigerate 3 hours or overnight.
2 Cook lamb, in batches, on heated oiled grill plate or barbecue until browned and cooked as desired. Serve with a mixed green salad and lemon wedges, if desired.

serves 4

spiced lamb and aubergine stack

800g lamb fillets, trimmed
3 teaspoons baharat spice blend
⅓ cup (80ml) olive oil
1 small (230g) aubergine, sliced
2 cloves garlic, crushed
2 bunches spinach, trimmed
½ cup (120g) aubergine dip
    (see page 6)
¼ cup (35g) semi-dried tomatoes,
    sliced

1 Sprinkle lamb with spice blend. Heat half the oil in a large frying pan. Cook lamb for about 7 minutes or until browned all over and cooked as desired. Transfer to a warmed plate; cover to keep warm.
2 In the same frying pan, heat remaining oil; cook the aubergine, in batches, over low heat, until tender. Add garlic, cook until fragrant. Remove from pan; set aside.
3 Meanwhile, bring water to boil in a saucepan. Add spinach; drain immediately.
4 Divide aubergine among serving plates; top with aubergine dip, sliced lamb, spinach and tomatoes. Serve with lemon wedges, if desired.

serves 4

chilli lamb couscous with spinach

¾ cup (180ml) olive oil
1½ teaspoons sugar
1 teaspoon sweet paprika
1 teaspoon ground cumin
1 small fresh red chilli, chopped finely
2 cloves garlic, crushed
salt and freshly ground black pepper
3 (600g) lamb loin fillets
⅓ cup (80ml) lemon juice
2 large (360g) carrots, sliced thinly
1½ cups (300g) couscous
1½ cups (375ml) boiling water
400g can chickpeas, rinsed, drained
75g baby spinach leaves
⅓ cup fresh mint, chopped finely
⅓ cup fresh coriander leaves

1 Reserve 1 tablespoon of the oil; combine remaining oil, sugar, paprika, cumin, chilli, garlic and salt and pepper to taste in a small screw-top jar; shake well. Place 2 tablespoons of the dressing in a medium bowl with lamb; cover, refrigerate for up to 3 hours. Add lemon juice to remaining dressing.
2 Boil, steam or microwave carrots until tender; drain. Place hot carrots in large serving bowl with half of the dressing; toss to coat.
3 Heat the reserved oil in a large frying pan. Cook lamb for about 10 minutes or until browned all over and cooked to medium. Transfer to a plate; cover to keep warm.
4 Meanwhile, place couscous in a large heatproof bowl; add boiling water and salt to taste. Stand, covered, for about 5 minutes or until water is absorbed. Fluff couscous with a fork.
5 Combine sliced lamb with remaining dressing, couscous, chickpeas, spinach and herbs in same bowl with carrots. Toss gently.

serves 6

Paprika is finely ground dried red pepper and is available in sweet, hot or smoked varieties.

Rigani is a type of oregano originally grown on the mountain slopes of Greece; the flower buds are used more so than the leaves.

meatballs with tomato and green olive salsa

4 slices (160g) white bread, crusts
    removed
⅓ cup (80ml) water
250g minced lamb
100g minced beef
2 (40g) spring onions, chopped finely
1 egg, beaten lightly
1 teaspoon grated lemon rind
1 teaspoon ground cumin
½ teaspoon dried rigani
salt and freshly ground black pepper
1 cup (150g) plain flour
olive or vegetable oil, for shallow-frying

tomato and green olive salsa
3 medium (450g) tomatoes, chopped
½ cup (50g) pitted green olives,
    chopped
1 tablespoon extra virgin olive oil
salt and freshly ground pepper to taste

1 Combine bread and water in a medium bowl, stand for 5 minutes. Using hands, squeeze excess water from bread.
2 Place minced meats, bread, onion, egg, rind, cumin, rigani, salt and pepper in a bowl; mix well. Cover; refrigerate for 1 hour.
3 Make tomato and green olive salsa.
4 With damp hands, roll mince mixture into 48 balls, about 2 teaspoons each. Roll balls in flour seasoned with salt and pepper; shake away excess flour.
5 Heat oil in frying pan, cook meatballs, in batches, for about 8 minutes, shaking pan frequently, or until browned and cooked through. Drain meatballs on kitchen paper. (If preparing meatballs ahead, cook until browned; drain on kitchen paper. Refrigerate. Before serving, place on an oven tray and bake for about 10 minutes or until cooked through and hot.)
6 Serve the meatballs with the tomato and green olive salsa.

tomato and green olive salsa Combine all the ingredients in a bowl.

makes *about 48*

cumin beef with kidney beans

1kg beef braising steak
2 tablespoons olive oil
2 medium onions (300g), finely
    chopped
2 cloves garlic, finely chopped
2 teaspoons ground oregano
1 teaspoon ground turmeric
2 teaspoons ground cumin
425g can tomatoes
2 cups (500ml) beef stock
¼ cup (60ml) tomato paste
2 bay leaves
1 cinnamon stick
6 baby new potatoes (240g), halved
2 small leeks (400g), thinly sliced
290g can kidney beans, rinsed, drained
2 tablespoons chopped fresh coriander
    leaves
2 tablespoons chopped fresh dill

1 Cut beef into 4cm pieces. Heat oil in pan, add beef in batches, cook, stirring, until browned. Transfer beef to ovenproof dish (2.5 litre/10 cup capacity).
2 Add onions to same pan, cook, stirring, until soft. Add garlic and ground spices, cook, stirring, until fragrant. Stir in undrained crushed tomatoes, stock and paste; bring to boil.
3 Pour tomato mixture over beef in dish, add bay leaves and cinnamon stick. Bake, covered, in moderately hot oven 1 hour.
4 Remove lid, bake for a further 30 minutes. Stir in potatoes and leeks. Bake, uncovered, for about 20 minutes more or until beef and potatoes are tender. Discard cinnamon and bay leaves. Stir in beans and herbs.

serves 6

beef with olives and coriander

1kg beef braising steak
50g ghee
2 medium onions (300g), finely
    chopped
2 teaspoons grated fresh ginger
½ teaspoon ground saffron
1 teaspoon ground cumin
1 teaspoon ground sweet paprika
1 tablespoon plain flour
¼ cup (60ml) lemon juice
2 cups (500ml) beef stock
1 tablespoon chopped fresh coriander
    leaves
1¼ cups (200g) pitted black olives
¾ cup (120g) pitted green olives

1 Cut beef into 3cm pieces. Heat ghee in pan, add beef in batches, cook, stirring, until browned all over; drain on kitchen paper.
2 Add onions and ginger to same pan, cook, stirring, until onions are soft.
3 Return beef to pan with saffron, cumin, paprika and flour, cook, stirring, until beef is well coated in spice mixture. Stir in juice and stock, simmer, covered, about 1½ hours or until beef is tender. Just before serving, stir in coriander and olives.

serves 6

Recipes for kofta — balls of seasoned minced meat — are included in some of the earliest known Arabic cookbooks.

kofta with spiced carrot salad

500g minced beef or lamb
1 cup (70g) fresh breadcrumbs
¼ cup finely chopped fresh mint
1 teaspoon ground allspice
1 teaspoon ground coriander
1 teaspoon cracked black pepper
1 tablespoon lemon juice
salt
200g plain yogurt

spiced carrot salad
3 large (540g) carrots
¼ cup (60ml) lemon juice
1 tablespoon olive oil
½ teaspoon ground cinnamon
½ teaspoon ground coriander
¼ cup firmly packed fresh mint leaves
¼ cup (35g) roasted shelled pistachios
¼ cup (40g) sultanas

1 Using your hands, combine minced meat, breadcrumbs, mint, spices, juice and salt in a medium bowl. Roll mixture into 12 balls, roll balls into sausage-shaped kofta. Cook kofta on a heated, oiled flat barbecue plate (or frying pan), uncovered, until cooked through.
2 Make spiced carrot salad.
3 Serve kofta with the spiced carrot salad and yogurt.

spiced carrot salad Cut carrots into 5cm lengths; slice pieces thinly lengthways. Cook carrot on a heated, oiled grill plate, uncovered, until just tender. Place carrot in a large bowl with remaining ingredients; toss gently to combine.

serves 4

spiced fried fish with lemon pistachio couscous

1 tablespoon plain flour
1½ teaspoons ground cumin
1½ teaspoons ground coriander
1 teaspoon sweet smoked paprika
¼ teaspoon cayenne pepper
8 (800g) sea bream fillets
1 tablespoon olive oil

lemon pistachio couscous
1 cup (200g) couscous
¾ cup (180ml) boiling water
2 teaspoons finely grated lemon rind
¼ cup (60ml) lemon juice
½ cup (70g) pistachios
2 teaspoons olive oil
1 clove garlic, crushed
1 small (100g) red onion, chopped
   finely
½ cup coarsely chopped fresh mint

1 Make lemon pistachio couscous
2 Combine flour and spices in a medium bowl; add fish, rub spice mixture over fish.
3 Heat oil in large non-stick frying pan; cook fish, in batches, until browned on both sides and cooked as desired.
4 Serve fish with lemon pistachio couscous and wedges of lemon, if desired.

lemon pistachio couscous Combine couscous, boiling water, lemon rind and juice in a medium heatproof bowl. Cover; stand about 5 minutes or until liquid is absorbed; fluff with a fork. Meanwhile, heat a small frying pan; dry-fry pistachios until fragrant. Remove nuts from pan. Heat oil in same pan, add garlic and onion; cook, stirring, until onion is soft. Stir nuts, onion mixture and mint through couscous. Cover to keep warm.

serves 4

We used sea bream in this recipe, but you can use any firm white fish fillet, such as cod, snapper or bass.

spiced fish with chickpeas and herbed couscous

4 x 150g firm white fish fillets
2 teaspoons ground turmeric
2 teaspoons ground cumin
1½ teaspoons ground cardamom
1½ tablespoons olive oil
1⅔ cups (410ml) chicken stock
2 x 300g cans chickpeas, rinsed,
    drained
2 medium red peppers (400g), sliced
¼ cup chopped fresh coriander leaves
1 tablespoon lemon juice

herbed couscous
1½ cups (300g) couscous
1 teaspoon olive oil
1½ cups (375ml) boiling water
1 tablespoon chopped fresh coriander
    leaves

1 Coat fish in combined spices.
2 Heat oil in pan, add fish, cook until browned on both sides and tender. Remove fish from pan; keep warm. Discard oil.
3 Add stock, chickpeas, peppers, coriander and juice to same pan, simmer, covered, about 10 minutes or until peppers are soft.
4 Meanwhile, make herbed couscous.
5 Serve fish on herbed couscous with chickpea mixture.

herbed couscous Place couscous in medium heatproof bowl, stir in oil, water and coriander; stand 5 minutes or until liquid is absorbed.

serves 4

whole fish with roasted tomatoes, peppers and olives

2 tablespoons extra virgin olive oil
1 medium (170g) red onion, cut into
    thick wedges
2 medium (400g) red peppers, sliced
    thickly
250g cherry tomatoes
4 cloves garlic, unpeeled, bruised
1kg whole snapper
sea salt and freshly ground black
    pepper
1 cup (120g) green olives
¼ cup coarsely chopped fresh flat-leaf
    parsley
lemon wedges, to serve

1 Preheat the oven to hot (220°C/200°C fan-assisted).
2 Combine half the olive oil with the onion, pepper, tomatoes and garlic in a large baking dish; roast, uncovered, for 20 minutes.
3 Rinse snapper in cold water; pat dry with kitchen paper. Score snapper diagonally on both sides. Season well with salt and pepper. Place snapper in same baking dish on top of the vegetables, drizzle with the remaining olive oil. Roast, uncovered, for a further 20 minutes or until fish is just cooked through.
4 Remove the fish from the oven and transfer to a platter. Sprinkle the green olives over the vegetables in the roasting dish; toss to combine.
5 Serve snapper over roasted vegetable mixture with parsley and lemon wedges.

serves 4

tip We used snapper in this recipe, but any firm white fish, such as bream or or bass, can be substituted.

pan-fried fish with spiced couscous

1 cup (250ml) salt-reduced chicken
    stock
1 cup (200g) couscous
20g butter
1 clove garlic, crushed
1 fresh long red chilli, sliced thinly
3 spring onions, sliced thinly
8 (800g) sea bream fillets, skin on
1 teaspoon ground cumin
1 teaspoon ground coriander
½ teaspoon sweet paprika
½ teaspoon salt
1 tablespoon olive oil
1 lemon, cut into wedges
1 tablespoon finely chopped fresh
    flat-leaf parsley

1 Microwave stock in a medium heatproof bowl on HIGH (100%) for about 1 minute or until boiling. Sprinkle couscous over stock; stand, covered, for 5 minutes. Fluff the couscous using a fork.
2 Meanwhile, heat the butter in a large non-stick frypan; cook garlic, chilli and onion, stirring, until fragrant. Add the couscous; cook, stirring with a whisk, until grains are separate and heated through. Transfer the couscous to a large bowl; cover to keep warm.
3 Pat fish dry with kitchen paper. Sprinkle both sides of fish with the combined spices and salt. Heat the oil in same frypan; cook fish until lightly browned on both sides and just cooked through.
4 Serve the fish with the couscous and lemon wedges; sprinkle with parsley.

serves 4

Middle Eastern food tends to be highly spiced and, while this recipe only uses one chilli, you can increase or decrease the quantity as you like.

baked fish with tomato and herb salad

2 tablespoons olive oil

2 large onions (400g), chopped coarsely

6 cloves garlic, chopped finely

1 fresh small red chilli, chopped finely

4 drained anchovy fillets, chopped finely

¾ cup coarsely chopped fresh flat-leaf parsley

1 cup coarsely chopped fresh coriander

¾ cup coarsely chopped fresh mint

200g mushrooms, quartered

2 trimmed celery stalks (200g), sliced thickly

2 teaspoons ground cumin

2 x 425g cans diced tomatoes

4 white fish cutlets (1kg)

1 medium lemon (140g), cut into wedges

2 tablespoons fresh flat-leaf parsley leaves

tomato and herb salad

5 medium tomatoes (750g), coarsely chopped

2 tablespoons coarsely chopped fresh mint

¼ cup coarsely chopped fresh flat-leaf parsley

2 tablespoons coarsely chopped fresh dill

2 cloves crushed garlic

2 tablespoons lemon juice

1 tablespoon olive oil

2 teaspoons white vinegar

1 Preheat oven to 200°C/180°C fan-assisted.

2 Heat oil in large deep flameproof baking dish; cook onion, garlic and chilli, stirring, until onion softens. Add anchovy, chopped herbs, mushrooms, celery and cumin; cook, stirring, 5 minutes.

3 Add undrained tomatoes; bring to a boil. Add fish; submerge it in tomato mixture. Return to a boil then cook, uncovered, in oven about 20 minutes or until liquid has almost evaporated and fish is cooked as desired.

4 Meanwhile, make tomato and herb salad.

5 Divide fish and lemon wedges among serving plates; sprinkle with parsley leaves. Serve with salad and, if desired, steamed white long-grain rice.

tomato and herb salad Combine tomatoes and herbs in medium bowl, drizzle with combined garlic, juice, oil and vinegar; toss gently.

serves 4

vegetables and salads

roast goats' cheese, pea and mint salad

½ cup (80g) shelled fresh peas
4 small (150g) pale celery stalks, sliced thinly
½ cup loosely packed young celery leaves
1 small frisee lettuce, trimmed
1 small radicchio, leaves separated
3 medium red radishes, sliced thinly
1 medium (150g) red apple, sliced thinly
½ cup loosely packed fresh mint leaves
220g goats' cheese, sliced (see note
   opposite)

honey mustard dressing
1 teaspoon wholegrain mustard
1 tablespoon lemon juice
1 tablespoon honey
1 tablespoon olive oil
salt and freshly ground black pepper to taste

1 Boil, steam or microwave the peas until just tender; drain. Refresh under cold water, drain.
2 Meanwhile, make honey mustard dressing.
3 Combine the peas with the remaining ingredients in a large bowl.
4 Just before serving, drizzle with honey mustard dressing.

honey mustard dressing Combine all the ingredients in a screw-top jar; shake well.

serves 4

We used ashed goat's cheese for this recipe, available from delicatessens and good supermarkets.

roasted pumpkin, carrots and parsnips

900g piece pumpkin, unpeeled,
  sliced thinly
1 tablespoon olive oil
4 large carrots (720g), halved, sliced
  thickly
2 large parsnips (700g), chopped
  coarsely
⅓ cup firmly packed fresh flat-leaf
  parsley leaves
¼ cup (40g) toasted pine nuts

spice paste
2 cloves garlic, quartered
1 teaspoon cumin seeds
1 teaspoon coriander seeds
½ teaspoon ground cinnamon
1 teaspoon sea salt
1 tablespoon olive oil
20g butter
¼ cup (55g) firmly packed
  brown sugar
1½ cups (375ml) apple juice

1 Preheat oven to moderately hot.
2 Place pumpkin and oil in large baking dish;
toss pumpkin to coat in oil. Roast, uncovered, in
moderately hot oven about 25 minutes or until
just tender.
3 Meanwhile, boil, steam or microwave carrot and
parsnip, separately, until just tender; drain. Make
spice paste.
4 Place vegetables, parsley and nuts in large bowl
with spice mixture; toss gently to combine.

spice paste Using mortar and pestle or small
electric spice blender, crush garlic, cumin, coriander,
cinnamon, salt and oil until mixture forms a thick
paste. Melt butter in large frying pan; cook paste,
stirring, about 3 minutes or until fragrant. Add sugar
and juice; bring to a boil. Cook, stirring, about
10 minutes or until spice mixture thickens slightly.

serves 8

Butternut squash, another member of the gourd family,
can be substituted for the pumpkin in this recipe.

spicy potato and coriander salad

1kg baby new potatoes, halved
1½ tablespoons olive oil
1 medium red onion (170g), chopped
3 cloves garlic, crushed
3 teaspoons ground cumin
1½ teaspoons ground coriander
1 teaspoon ground sweet paprika
½ teaspoon ground turmeric
¼ teaspoon ground cinnamon
½ cup chopped fresh coriander leaves

dressing
⅓ cup (80ml) lemon juice
¼ cup (60ml) olive oil
½ teaspoon sambal oelek
1 teaspoon sugar
¼ teaspoon cracked black pepper

1 Add potatoes to pan of boiling water, simmer, uncovered, until tender; drain.
2 Heat oil in pan, add onion, garlic and ground spices, cook, stirring, until onion is soft. Add potatoes and coriander, cook, stirring, about 5 minutes or until potatoes are well coated and heated through. Combine potato mixture and dressing in bowl; mix well.

dressing Place all ingredients in jar; shake well.

serves 4 to 6

marinated lamb salad with lemon yogurt dressing

750g lamb loin fillet
2 cloves garlic, crushed
1 tablespoon finely chopped fresh mint leaves
1 tablespoon finely shredded lemon rind
2 tablespoons lemon juice
2 medium (400g) red peppers
1 cucumber, sliced thinly
1 medium (170g) red onion, sliced thinly
100g pitted black olives
100g feta cheese, crumbled
1 baby cos lettuce

lemon yogurt dressing
200ml plain yogurt
¼ cup (60ml) lemon juice
1 clove garlic, crushed
2 tablespoons water

1 Combine lamb with garlic, mint, rind and juice in large shallow dish; cover, refrigerate 3 hours or overnight.
2 Drain lamb; discard marinade. Cook lamb in heated oiled grill pan (or on grill or barbecue) until browned all over and cooked as desired. Cover lamb, rest 5 minutes; slice thinly.
3 Cut peppers into diamond shapes.
4 Gently toss lamb, pepper, cucumber, onion, olives, cheese and lettuce leaves in large bowl with dressing.

lemon yogurt dressing Whisk ingredients together in small bowl.

serves 4

Harissa, a traditional spice paste used throughout North Africa and the Middle East, is made from dried chillies, garlic, olive oil and caraway seeds. It can be used as a rub for meat, an ingredient in sauces and dressings, or eaten on its own as a condiment.

roasted vegetables with harissa yoghurt

1.2kg pumpkin or butternut squash
3 medium (500g) beetroot, halved
2 medium (500g) parsnips, peeled,
    halved lengthways
1 bunch (400g) baby carrots, trimmed
2 medium (320g) red onions, halved
2 tablespoons olive oil
50g butter, chopped
salt
1 cup (280g) Greek-style plain yogurt
1 tablespoon harissa

1 Preheat the oven to hot (220°C/200°C fan-assisted).
2 Cut pumpkin into thin wedges. Place all vegetables in two large baking dishes; drizzle with oil and dot with butter. Sprinkle with a little salt.
3 Roast the vegetables for 40 minutes, turning once. Remove vegetables as they are cooked; return trays to oven for a further 10 minutes or until all vegetables are browned and tender.
4 Meanwhile, combine yogurt and harissa in a small bowl. Serve roasted vegetables with harissa yogurt.

serves 6

grilled aubergine with tabbouleh

3 small tomatoes (270g)
¼ cup (40g) bulgar wheat
2 large aubergines (1kg)
⅓ cup (80ml) extra virgin olive oil
4 cups coarsely chopped fresh flat-leaf
   parsley
1 cup coarsely chopped fresh mint
1 medium red onion (170g), chopped
   finely
2 tablespoons lemon juice

1 Chop tomatoes finely, retaining as much juice as possible. Place tomato and juice on top of the bulgar wheat in small bowl; cover, refrigerate 2 hours or until bulgar is soft.
2 Cut each aubergine into 8 wedges. Brush aubergine with half the oil; cook on heated grill plate (or grill or barbecue) about 10 minutes or until browned and tender.
3 Meanwhile, combine tomato mixture with the parsley, mint, onion, juice and remaining oil.
4 Serve tabbouleh with aubergine.

serves 4

green olive chicken salad

1 large (750g) cos lettuce, shredded
   finely
3 cups (480g) cooked chicken,
   shredded finely
6 spring onions, sliced thinly
¼ cup (30g) pitted green olives, sliced
   thinly
2 tablespoons fresh dill, chopped
⅓ cup (80ml) olive oil
¼ cup (60ml) lemon juice
salt and freshly ground black pepper

1 Combine the lettuce, chicken, onions, olives and dill in a large serving bowl.
2 Combine oil, juice and salt and pepper to taste in a screw-top jar; shake well.
3 Just before serving, add the dressing to the salad and toss gently to combine. Serve with grilled or fresh bread, if desired.

serves 6
tip *You will need a large barbecued chicken for this recipe.*

74

orange, date and almond salad

4 large oranges (1.2kg)
⅓ cup (50g) dried apricots, halved
2 tablespoons blanched almonds, toasted
2 tablespoons chopped fresh mint

syrup mixture
1 cup (250ml) water
2 star anise
1 cinnamon stick
6 cloves
2 tablespoons honey
½ cup (95g) sliced dried figs
½ cup (85g) stoned dates, halved

1 Peel oranges thickly, remove any white pith, cut between membranes into segments.
2 Combine orange segments, apricots, almonds and mint in bowl, add syrup mixture; mix well.

syrup mixture Combine water, star anise, cinnamon, cloves and honey in small pan, simmer, uncovered, about 10 minutes or until thickened and slightly syrupy. Add figs and dates; cool. Discard star anise, cinnamon and cloves.

serves 4

tomato, feta and spring onion salad

500g feta cheese
4 medium (500g) tomatoes
⅓ cup (80ml) olive oil
¼ cup (60ml) lemon juice
3 spring onions, finely chopped
2 tablespoons chopped fresh mint

topping
2 tablespoons roughly chopped walnuts, toasted
3 teaspoons sesame seeds, toasted
¼ teaspoon cumin seeds
¼ teaspoon coriander seeds

1 Cut cheese into 1cm pieces. Cut tomatoes into wedges, remove seeds and cores; chop flesh finely.
2 Whisk oil and juice in small bowl until combined; add onions and mint; mix well.
3 Combine half mint mixture with tomatoes in bowl; gently stir to combine. Combine remaining mint mixture with cheese in separate bowl; gently stir to combine. Refrigerate tomato mixture and cheese mixture, covered, at least 1 hour. Place cheese mixture on serving plate, sprinkle with half the topping, top with tomato mixture, then add the remaining topping.

topping Finely chop nuts and seeds; combine well.

serves 4 to 6

roasted aubergine with spiced rice

3 medium aubergines (900g)
⅓ cup (80ml) extra virgin olive oil
2 cloves garlic, sliced thinly
1 tablespoon extra virgin olive oil, extra
1 tablespoon finely chopped fresh
   flat-leaf parsley
1 tablespoon finely chopped fresh mint

spiced rice
30g butter
1 medium onion (150g), chopped finely
1 clove garlic, crushed
3 cardamom pods, bruised
½ cinnamon stick
2 cups (400g) basmati rice
1 cup (250ml) vegetable stock
1 cup (250ml) water
¼ cup (40g) toasted pine nuts

1 Preheat oven to 220°C/200°C fan-assisted.
2 Cut aubergines into 3cm slices crossways; discard ends. Heat one-third of the oil in large frying pan; cook one-third of the aubergines until browned on both sides. Transfer to large shallow baking dish. Repeat with remaining oil and aubergine slices.
3 Sprinkle aubergine with garlic; bake, in oven, about 20 minutes or until aubergine is tender.
4 Meanwhile, make spiced rice.
5 Drizzle aubergine with extra oil; top with parsley and mint. Serve with spiced rice.

spiced rice Melt butter in medium saucepan. Add onion, garlic, cardamom and cinnamon; cook, stirring, without browning, until onion is softened. Add rice; stir to coat in butter mixture. Stir in stock and the water; bring to a boil then simmer, covered, about 15 minutes or until stock is absorbed. Remove from heat; stand, covered, 5 minutes. Stir in nuts.

serves 4

Cooks used to salt aubergines to remove bitterness and moisture. Today's aubergines are rarely bitter, but salting can help reduce the amount of oil they absorb during cooking. Cut the aubergine into slices, sprinkle with salt and stand in a colander for about 30 minutes to allow the juices to drain away. Rinse and dry well before use.

layered aubergine and pepper salad

3 medium red peppers (600g)
1kg (about 16) finger aubergines
⅓ cup (80ml) olive oil
⅓ cup (50g) chopped pistachios, toasted

herby yogurt dressing
1 cup (250ml) plain yogurt
1 clove garlic, crushed
¼ cup chopped fresh coriander leaves
1½ tablespoons chopped fresh oregano
1 teaspoon ground cumin
2 teaspoons honey

1 Quarter peppers, remove seeds and membranes. Grill peppers, skin side up, until skin blisters and blackens. Peel away skin, slice flesh thickly.
2 Cut aubergines in half lengthways. Heat 1 tablespoon of the oil in pan, add a third of the aubergines to pan, cook about 10 minutes, or until browned all over and very soft; drain on absorbent paper. Repeat with remaining oil and aubergines.
3 Spread quarter of the yogurt dressing onto serving plate; top with a third of the aubergines, then a third of the peppers. Repeat layering twice more. Top with remaining yogurt dressing; sprinkle with nuts.

herby yogurt dressing Combine all ingredients in bowl; mix well.

serves *6 to 8*

beetroot and orange salad

3 x 400g jar mini baby beets, drained
1 cup fresh flat-leaf parsley, chopped coarsely
1 medium orange (240g), peeled, segmented
2 tablespoons red wine vinegar
2 tablespoons extra virgin olive oil

1 Combine beets, parsley and orange segments in medium bowl.
2 Combine vinegar and olive oil in screw-top jar; shake well.
3 Just before serving, add dressing to salad; toss gently to mix.

serves *8*

spinach salad with bulgar wheat and chickpeas

1 large red pepper (350g)
1 cup (160g) bulgar wheat
1 cup (250ml) boiling water
420g can chickpeas, rinsed, drained
1 trimmed celery stalk (100g), chopped
    finely
50g baby spinach leaves

sumac and herb dressing
1 tablespoon sesame seeds
2 tablespoons sumac
1 tablespoon fresh thyme leaves
1 tablespoon coarsely chopped fresh
    oregano
½ cup (125ml) lime juice
1 tablespoon olive oil
1 clove garlic, crushed

1 Quarter pepper; discard seeds and membranes. Roast under grill or in very hot oven, skin-side up, until skin blisters and blackens. Cover pepper pieces with plastic or paper for 5 minutes; peel away skin then slice flesh thinly.
2 Meanwhile, place bulgar wheat in medium bowl, cover with the boiling water; stand about 10 minutes or until bulgar softens and water is absorbed.
3 Combine ingredients for sumac and herb dressing in small bowl.
4 Place bulgar wheat and pepper in large bowl with chickpeas, celery, spinach and dressing; toss gently.

serves 4

beetroot, fennel and lentil salad

3 medium beetroot (1.5kg), trimmed
1 tablespoon olive oil
1 medium fennel bulb (300g)
400g can brown lentils, rinsed, drained
100g wild rocket leaves
200g feta cheese, sliced thinly

fennel dressing
½ cup (125ml) olive oil
2 tablespoons lemon juice
½ teaspoon white sugar
2 teaspoons finely chopped fresh
    fennel fronds

1 Preheat oven to 180°C/160°C fan-assisted.
2 Combine beetroot in small baking dish with oil. Bake about 1 hour or until tender. When cool, peel beetroot then chop coarsely.
3 Finely chop enough of the fennel fronds to give the 2 teaspoons needed for the dressing. Slice fennel bulb thinly.
4 Combine dressing ingredients in screw-top jar; shake well.
5 Toss fennel, lentils and rocket in large bowl with half the dressing. Add beetroot; toss gently. Top with feta; drizzle with remaining dressing.

serves 6
tip *Beetroot and dressing can be prepared a day ahead.*

couscous and rice

almond coriander couscous

3 cups (600g) couscous
3 cups (750ml) boiling water
¼ cup (60ml) olive oil
1 clove garlic, crushed
2 spring onions, chopped
¾ cup (105g) slivered almonds, toasted
⅓ cup (50g) currants
½ cup chopped fresh coriander leaves

1 Combine couscous and water in bowl, stand 5 minutes or until water is absorbed. Fluff couscous with fork.
2 Heat oil in large pan, add garlic and onions, cook, stirring, until onions are soft. Add couscous to pan, stir over heat until heated through.
3 Stir nuts, currants and coriander into couscous mixture.

serves 6

fruity rice

50g ghee
1½ cups (300g) basmati rice
3 cups (750ml) water
250g fresh dates, stoned, thinly sliced
2 teaspoons orange flower water
½ cup (75g) dried apricots, thinly sliced
2 tablespoons chopped fresh parsley

1 Heat ghee in medium heavy-based pan, add rice, cook, stirring, until rice is coated with ghee. Add water, simmer, covered with tight-fitting lid, 12 minutes. Remove pan from heat, stand, covered, 10 minutes.
2 Add remaining ingredients to rice mixture and stir well.

serves 4 to 6

A staple of Middle-Eastern cuisine, couscous is made from rolled, shaped grains of semolina wheat with a coating of finely ground wheat flour.

vegetable rice with chickpeas

1 tablespoon olive oil
1 large onion (200g), chopped
3 cloves garlic, crushed
1 teaspoon sambal oelek
2 teaspoons ground cumin
½ teaspoon ground cinnamon
1 teaspoon ground ginger
425g can tomatoes
150g baby yellow squash, quartered
2 tablespoons chopped fresh parsley
2 tablespoons chopped fresh coriander leaves
3 cups cooked white long-grain rice
2 x 425g cans chickpeas, rinsed, drained
¼ cup (60ml) orange juice

1 Heat oil in large pan, add onion, garlic, sambal oelek and spices, cook, stirring, until onion is soft.
2 Add undrained crushed tomatoes, squash and herbs, simmer, uncovered, until squash are tender.
3 Add rice, chickpeas and juice, cook, stirring, until heated through.

serves 6

tip *You will need to cook 1 cup (200g) long-grain rice for this recipe.*

saffron orange rice with pine nuts

2 tablespoons olive oil
1 clove garlic, crushed
1 large onion (200g), chopped
¼ teaspoon saffron threads
2 teaspoons grated orange rind
½ teaspoon ground cinnamon
1 teaspoon ground cumin
2 cups (400g) basmati rice
1 litre (4 cups) chicken stock
¼ cup (35g) currants
2 tablespoons chopped fresh parsley
⅓ cup (50g) pine nuts, toasted

1 Heat oil in pan, add garlic and onion, cook, stirring, until onion is just soft. Add saffron, rind and spices.
2 Add rice, stir over heat until rice is coated with oil. Stir in stock, simmer, covered with tight-fitting lid, 12 minutes.
3 Remove from heat; stand, covered, for 10 minutes. Stir in currants and parsley; sprinkle with nuts. Top with shredded orange rind, if desired.

serves 6

desserts

honey and yoghurt mousse

500g plain Greek yogurt
½ cup (175g) honey
¾ cup (180ml) double cream
1 vanilla pod, halved lengthways
   (or 1 teaspoon vanilla bean paste)
1 teaspoon gelatine
1 tablespoon water
2 egg whites
2 tablespoons caster sugar

honey muscatels
½ cup (125ml) water
½ cup (90g) honey
50g muscatels (see note opposite)

1 Place yogurt in a sieve lined with muslin. Place sieve over a bowl, cover and refrigerate overnight.
2 Combine honey, cream and vanilla pod in a medium saucepan; stir over low heat until honey is dissolved, remove from heat.
3 Meanwhile, sprinkle gelatine over the measured water in a small heatproof jug; place in a small saucepan of simmering water until gelatine dissolves. Stir gelatine into honey mixture, cool until lukewarm; remove vanilla pod. Stir yogurt into honey mixture until combined well.
4 Beat egg whites until firm peaks form, add sugar, beat until dissolved. Fold egg whites into honey and yogurt mixture. Pour mixture into 6 x ¾-cup (180ml) serving glasses; cover, refrigerate for about 3 hours or until set.
5 Meanwhile, make honey muscatels.
6 Serve mousses topped with honey muscatels and drizzled with syrup.

honey muscatels Place measured water, honey and muscatels in a small saucepan; bring to the boil. Simmer, uncovered, for about 5 minutes or until syrup has thickened. Cool.

serves 6

Muscatels are large dried grapes on the stem,
available from gourmet food stores and some
health food stores.

glacé fruit and citrus frozen puddings with bitter orange sauce

1½ cups (280g) finely chopped mixed glacé fruit
½ cup (170g) orange marmalade
2 tablespoons orange juice
2 teaspoons finely grated orange rind
¼ cup coarsely chopped fresh mint
2 litres vanilla ice-cream, slightly softened

bitter orange sauce
⅔ cup (160ml) orange juice
⅓ cup (115g) orange marmalade
2 tablespoons lemon juice

1 Line eight 1-cup (250ml) moulds with cling film.
2 Combine fruit, marmalade, juice, rind and mint in medium bowl.
3 Place ice-cream in large bowl; fold in fruit mixture. Divide mixture among prepared moulds; cover with foil. Freeze puddings 3 hours or overnight.
4 Make bitter orange sauce.
5 Turn puddings out of moulds onto serving plates; serve with bitter orange sauce.

bitter orange sauce Combine ingredients in small jug.

serves 8

almond cream with spiced fruit

¼ cup (35g) rice flour
¼ cup (55g) caster sugar
3 cups (750ml) milk
½ teaspoon grated lemon rind
¾ cup (90g) ground almonds
¼ cup (35g) slivered almonds
1 tablespoon rosewater

spiced fruit
½ cup (45g) dried apples
¾ cup (110g) dried apricots
½ cup (85g) pitted prunes
1 litre (4 cups) water
¾ cup (165g) caster sugar
2 cinnamon sticks
3 cloves
1 tablespoon rosewater
¼ cup (30g) chopped walnuts

1 Blend rice flour and sugar with ½ cup (125ml) of the milk in small bowl. Bring remaining milk and rind to boil in medium pan, stir in flour mixture, stir constantly over heat until mixture boils and thickens.
2 Stir in remaining ingredients. Spoon mixture into 6 dishes (¾ cup/180ml capacity); cool. Cover, refrigerate until cold. Serve with spiced fruit.

spiced fruit Place fruit in bowl, cover with water; stand 2 hours. Drain, discard water. Bring measured water, sugar, cinnamon, cloves and rosewater to boil in pan, simmer, uncovered, 30 minutes or until syrupy and reduced to about 2½ cups (625ml). Remove from heat, stir in fruit and nuts, cool. Cover; refrigerate 3 hours or overnight.

serves 6

baked rice pudding with poached quinces

1.25 litres (5 cups) water
1kg (5 cups) caster sugar
4 medium quinces (1.5kg), peeled,
    cored, quartered
10cm strip lemon rind
1 tablespoon lemon juice
1 cinnamon stick, halved
½ cup (100g) white medium-grain rice
2¾ cups (680ml) milk
300ml double cream
⅓ cup (75g) caster sugar, extra
1 teaspoon vanilla extract
½ cup (75g) caramelised almonds,
    chopped coarsely

1 Combine the water and sugar in large pan; stir over medium heat without boiling, until sugar dissolves; bring to a boil. Add quince, rind, juice and half cinnamon stick; simmer, covered, about 2 hours or until quince are rosy and tender.
2 Preheat oven to 150°C/130°C fan-assisted.
3 Place rice in sieve; rinse under cold water until water runs clear, drain.
4 Place rice, milk, cream, extra sugar, extract and remaining half cinnamon stick in small baking dish; stir. Bake, uncovered, about 2 hours or until tender, stirring every 30 minutes.
5 Serve rice with quince and a little of the syrup; sprinkle with nuts.

serves 4

cinnamon rice pudding

1 litre (4 cups) milk
⅓ cup (75g) caster sugar
5cm piece orange rind
½ cup (100g) short-grain rice
1 tablespoon custard powder
¼ cup (60ml) milk, extra
ground cinnamon

1 Combine milk, sugar and rind in saucepan, stirring constantly over heat, without boiling, until sugar is dissolved.
2 Bring to boil, add rice; simmer, uncovered, 30 minutes or until rice is tender, stirring occasionally.
3 Remove rind, stir in blended custard powder and extra milk; stir over heat until mixture boils and thickens. Pour mixture into four serving dishes, sprinkle with cinnamon. Serve warm or cold.

serves 4

spiced fruits

baked spiced quinces

6 medium quinces (2kg)
1 medium orange (180g)
1 litre (4 cups) boiling water
2 cups (440g) caster sugar
2 vanilla pods, split
4 cardamom pods, crushed
1 cinnamon stick
1 tablespoon honey
½ cup (125ml) orange juice

1 Peel and halve quinces, cut each half into four pieces; remove core.
2 Peel four thin pieces of rind from orange using a vegetable peeler. Cut pieces of rind into very thin strips.
3 Combine boiling water and sugar in jug, stir until sugar is dissolved. Place quinces in large shallow ovenproof dish (4.5 litre/18 cup capacity). Add rind, vanilla pods, cardamom and cinnamon. Pour sugar syrup over quinces.
4 Bake quinces, covered, in moderately hot oven about 2 hours or until quinces are changed in colour, tender and liquid is syrupy. Carefully remove quinces to large bowl. Stir honey and juice into syrup mixture in dish; pour over quinces in bowl, cover; refrigerate 3 hours or overnight. Remove cinnamon and vanilla pods.

serves *6 to 8*

fresh peaches and dates with orange flower water

½ cup (125ml) water
½ cup (125ml) caster sugar
pinch saffron threads
4 cardamom pods
⅓ cup (80ml) lemon juice
1 teaspoon orange flower water
6 large peaches (1.5kg), sliced thickly
12 fresh dates (250g), quartered
1 cup (280g) plain yogurt

1 Combine the water, sugar, saffron and cardamom in small saucepan; stir over low heat, without boiling, until sugar is dissolved. Bring to boil; simmer, uncovered, about 5 minutes or until mixture just thickens. Cool 10 minutes. Stir in juice and orange flower water.
2 Place peaches and dates in large bowl; strain syrup over fruit. Refrigerate 2 hours.
3 Serve fruit with yogurt.

serves *8*

honey-grilled plums and figs

8 small plums (600g), halved, stoned
6 medium figs (360g), halved
⅓ cup (115g) honey
2 tablespoons brown sugar
⅔ cup (190g) plain yogurt

1 Preheat grill.
2 Place plums and figs on shallow baking tray; drizzle with half the honey, sprinkle with sugar. Grill until browned lightly and just tender.
3 Divide fruit among serving plates, drizzle with remaining honey and juices in baking tray. Serve with yogurt.

serves 4

poached nectarines

3 cups (750g) water
1 cup (220g) caster sugar
1 star anise
10cm strip orange rind
8 small nectarines (800g)
⅔ cup (190g) plain yogurt

1 Combine the water, sugar, star anise and rind in medium saucepan, stir over medium heat until sugar dissolves; bring to a boil. Boil, uncovered, 2 minutes. Add nectarines; simmer, uncovered, 20 minutes. Cool nectarines 10 minutes in poaching liquid.
2 Using slotted spoon, transfer nectarines to serving dishes; bring liquid to a boil. Boil, uncovered, about 5 minutes or until syrup reduces to 1 cup; strain into small bowl.
3 Cool syrup to room temperature; pour ¼ cup of the syrup over nectarines in each dish; serve with yogurt and almond bread.

serves 4

Although not a juicy fruit, fresh figs are incredibly luscious, with a sweet, delicate flavour.

poached plums with almond milk ice-cream

2 cups (500ml) water
½ cup (70g) roasted slivered almonds
1 vanilla pod
300ml double cream
¾ cup (165g) caster sugar
6 egg yolks

poached plums
2 cups (500ml) water
1 cup (250ml) pomegranate juice
½ cup (110g) caster sugar
1 cinnamon stick
4 plums (450g), halved, stoned

1 Line 14cm x 21cm loaf tin with baking parchment.
2 Blend or process the water and nuts until fine. Strain almond milk through muslin-lined strainer into medium saucepan; discard solids.
3 Halve vanilla pod lengthways, scrape seeds into pan with almond milk. Add pod, cream and ¼ cup of the sugar to pan; bring to a boil. Remove from heat; stand 30 minutes. Discard pod.
4 Beat egg yolks and remaining sugar in medium bowl with electric mixer until thick and creamy. Gradually stir in almond milk mixture; return to pan. Cook, stirring, over low heat, until mixture thickens slightly. Remove from heat; cool to room temperature. Pour ice-cream mixture into loaf tin, cover with foil; freeze until firm.
5 Remove ice-cream from freezer, turn into large bowl; chop ice-cream coarsely then beat with electric mixer until smooth. Return to loaf tin, cover; freeze until firm.
6 Meanwhile, make poached plums.
7 Cut ice-cream into four slices; divide among serving plates. Top with plums and syrup.

poached plums Stir the water, juice, sugar and cinnamon in medium saucepan, without boiling, until sugar dissolves. Add plums; cook, uncovered, over low heat, about 30 minutes or until just tender. Remove plums from syrup; discard skins. Bring syrup to a boil; boil, uncovered, about 10 minutes or until syrup is reduced to about 1 cup. Remove from heat, discard cinnamon; cool 10 minutes. Refrigerate, covered, until cold.

serves 4

sweets, pastries and drinks

almond shortbread

250g unsalted butter, chopped
1 teaspoon vanilla extract
½ cup (80g) icing sugar, sifted
1 egg yolk
1 tablespoon orange flower water
½ cup (70g) finely chopped toasted flaked
  almonds
2 cups (300g) plain flour
½ cup (75g) self-raising flour
icing sugar, to coat, extra

1 Beat butter, vanilla and sugar in a small bowl with an electric mixer until light and fluffy. Beat in egg yolk and orange flower water. Transfer mixture to a large bowl; stir in almonds and combined sifted flours.

2 Preheat oven to moderately low (160°C/ 140°C fan-assisted).

3 Take a level tablespoon of dough and roll between palms into sausage shape, tapering at ends; bend into a crescent. Repeat with remaining dough. Place on lightly greased baking trays, 3cm apart. Bake for about 15 to 20 minutes or until browned lightly. Cool on baking trays for 5 minutes.

4 Sift a thick layer of the extra icing sugar onto a large sheet of baking parchment. Place shortbreads on icing sugar, dust tops of shortbreads heavily with icing sugar. Cool. Pack into an airtight container, sifting more icing sugar onto each layer. Store at room temperature for up to 1 week.

5 Serve with cardamom coffee (see page 108), if desired.

makes about 32

Orange flower water is often used in
Middle-eastern cooking for its cooling
effect and delicate, fragrant aroma.

honey cookies

125g butter
2 teaspoons grated lemon rind
⅓ cup (75g) caster sugar
⅓ cup (80ml) vegetable oil
2 cups (300g) plain flour
1 cup (150g) self-raising flour
¼ cup (30g) chopped walnuts
⅓ cup (160ml) orange juice
1 cup (250ml) honey
2 tablespoons chopped walnuts, extra
2 teaspoons sesame seeds

1 Preheat oven to moderate. Lightly grease two oven trays.
2 Cream butter, rind and sugar in small bowl with electric mixer until combined. Gradually beat in oil until mixture is light and fluffy.
3 Transfer mixture to large bowl, stir in sifted flours, nuts and juice in two batches; mix to a soft dough.
4 Roll level tablespoons of mixture into egg shapes; place on prepared trays, flatten slightly. Mark biscuits lightly with fork. Bake in moderate oven 20 minutes or until browned. Stand biscuits on trays 5 minutes before placing on wire rack to cool.
5 Heat honey in pan until just warm; dip biscuits in honey to coat, place on wire rack over tray. Sprinkle with combined extra nuts and seeds.

makes about 40

honey walnut puffs

2 teaspoons (7g) dried yeast
1 cup (250ml) warm milk
2 tablespoons caster sugar
1 egg, beaten lightly
60g butter, melted
2 cups (300g) plain flour
oil for deep-frying
⅔ cup (160ml) honey
¼ teaspoon ground cinnamon
¼ cup (30g) chopped walnuts

1 Combine yeast, milk, sugar, egg and butter in large bowl; mix well. Gradually stir in sifted flour; beat until smooth.
2 Stand, covered, in a warm place 1½ hours or until batter doubles in size and bubbles appears on the surface. Beat batter until smooth.
3 Deep-fry level tablespoons of batter in hot oil, turning puffs to give an even colour; drain on absorbent paper.
4 Heat honey in pan until just warm. Place puffs on serving plate, drizzle with honey, sprinkle with cinnamon and nuts.

makes about 26

orange coconut cake

250g butter, chopped
1 tablespoon grated orange rind
¼ cup (55g) caster sugar
4 eggs
1 cup (150g) self-raising flour
¼ teaspoon baking powder
2 teaspoons ground cinnamon
1 cup (125g) ground almonds
1½ cups (135g) desiccated coconut
½ cup (60g) chopped pecans
¾ cup (180ml) orange juice
¼ cup (20g) flaked almonds

syrup
1 cup (220g) caster sugar
⅓ cup (160ml) orange juice

1 Grease deep 23cm round cake tin, line tin with baking parchment.
2 Beat butter, rind and sugar in small bowl with electric mixer until light and fluffy. Add eggs one at a time, beating well between additions.
3 Transfer mixture to large bowl. Stir in sifted flour, baking powder and cinnamon, ground almonds, coconut and pecans. Stir in juice.
4 Spread mixture into prepared tin, sprinkle with flaked almonds. Bake in moderate oven about 45 minutes. Pour hot syrup over hot cake in tin. Cool in tin.

syrup Combine sugar and juice in pan, stir over low heat, without boiling, until sugar is dissolved. Boil, uncovered, without stirring, about 5 minutes or until syrup is slightly thickened.

poppy seed cookies

200g butter, chopped
2 teaspoons grated lime rind
⅓ cup (75g) caster sugar
½ teaspoon ground cinnamon
2 teaspoons lime juice
1 tablespoon poppy seeds
1¾ cups (260g) plain flour
¼ cup (35g) macadamia nuts,
    quartered

1 Beat butter, rind, sugar and cinnamon in small bowl with electric mixer until just combined. Stir in juice and seeds, then sifted flour in two batches.
2 Divide mixture in half, roll each piece on floured surface to an 18cm sausage. Wrap in cling film, refrigerate until firm. Trim ends, cut into 8mm slices.
3 Place cookies about 2cm apart on greased oven trays; press nuts into centres. Bake in moderate oven about 12 minutes or until lightly browned. Stand 5 minutes, cool on wire racks.

makes *about 48*

fruit and nut cake

½ cup (115g) coarsely chopped
   glacé pineapple
½ cup (125g) coarsely chopped
   glacé apricots
1½ cups (250g) pitted dried dates
½ cup (110g) red glacé cherries
½ cup (110g) green glacé cherries
1 cup (170g) brazil nuts
½ cup (75g) macadamia nuts
2 eggs
½ cup (110g) firmly packed brown
   sugar
100g butter, melted
⅓ cup (50g) plain flour
¼ cup (35g) self-raising flour

fruit and nut topping
⅓ cup (75g) coarsely chopped glacé
   pineapple
¼ cup (55g) red glacé cherries, halved
¼ cup (55g) green glacé cherries,
   halved
¼ cup (40g) brazil nuts
¼ cup (35g) macadamia nuts

caramel topping
½ cup (110g) caster sugar
¼ cup (60ml) water

1 Preheat oven to low.
2 Grease 20cm-ring cake tin; line base and side with baking parchment, extending parchment 5cm above side.
3 Combine fruit and nuts in large bowl.
4 Beat eggs and sugar in small bowl with electric mixer until thick. Add butter and sifted flours; beat until just combined. Stir egg mixture into fruit mixture. Press mixture firmly into prepared tin.
5 Make fruit and nut topping. Gently press topping evenly over cake mixture; bake, covered, in low oven 1 hour. Uncover; bake in low oven about 45 minutes. Stand cake in tin 10 minutes.
6 Meanwhile, make toffee topping. Turn cake, top-side up, onto wire rack; drizzle with toffee topping.

fruit and nut topping Combine ingredients in medium bowl.

toffee topping Combine ingredients in small saucepan, stir over heat without boiling until sugar dissolves; bring to a boil. Reduce heat; simmer, uncovered, without stirring, about 10 minutes or until mixture is golden. Remove from heat; stand until bubbles subside before using.

tip *This cake can be baked in two 8cm x 26cm cake tins. Line bases and sides with baking parchment, extending parchment 5cm above long sides. Bake, covered, in low oven 1 hour; uncover, bake in low oven about 30 minutes.*

orange almond cookies

200g butter, chopped
1 tablespoon finely grated orange rind
1 cup (160g) icing sugar
2 teaspoons orange flower water
2 eggs, lightly beaten
2 cups (300g) plain flour
2½ cups (310g) ground almonds
¼ cup (40g) blanched almonds, halved

1 Beat butter, rind, sifted icing sugar and orange flower water in small bowl with electric mixer until light and fluffy. Add eggs gradually, beat until just combined. Transfer mixture to large bowl. Stir in sifted flour and ground nuts, mix to a soft dough. Wrap dough in cling film, refrigerate 30 minutes.
2 Roll tablespoons of mixture into balls. Place balls about 4cm apart on greased oven trays, flatten slightly, press halved nuts into centres. Bake cookies in moderate oven about 15 minutes or until lightly browned. Cool cookies on trays.

makes *about 45*

date and nut crescents

1⅔ cups (250g) plain flour
125g butter, chopped
¼ cup (60ml) iced water, approximately
icing sugar

filling
250g (about 10) fresh dates, stoned, chopped
⅓ cup (80ml) water
¼ cup (75g) walnuts, toasted, chopped
¼ teaspoon ground cinnamon

1 Sift flour into large bowl, rub in butter, gradually stir in enough water to mix to a firm dough. Knead dough on lightly floured surface about 5 minutes or until smooth, cover; refrigerate 1 hour.
2 Roll pastry on floured surface until 3mm thick, cut into 7cm rounds.
3 Brush edges of rounds with water, drop a teaspoon of filling into centre of each round, fold over to enclose filling; press edges together. Shape into crescents, place 2cm apart on greased oven trays. Bake in moderate oven about 20 minutes; cool on wire racks. Toss crescents in sifted icing sugar.

filling Combine dates and water in small pan, simmer, uncovered, about 5 minutes or until dates are softened. Stir in remaining ingredients; cool.

makes *about 40*

semolina slice

1kg (6¼ cups) coarsely ground
   semolina
2½ cups (550g) granulated white sugar
1 cup (250ml) milk
125g butter
¼ cup (40g) blanched almonds

sugar syrup
3 cups (750ml) water
2 teaspoons lemon juice
1½ cups (330g) caster sugar
2 teaspoons orange flower water

1 Make sugar syrup.
2 Preheat oven to 160°C/140°C fan-assisted. Grease 20cm x 30cm sturdy baking tin.
3 Combine semolina and sugar in large bowl. Combine milk and butter in small saucepan; stir over low heat until butter melts. Pour into semolina mixture; stir to combine.
4 Spread mixture into tin; smooth top. Score slice into 4cm diamond shapes; centre one nut on each diamond. Bake, uncovered, in oven about 1 hour 20 minutes or until slice is golden brown and slightly firm to the touch.
5 Cut through diamond shapes to bottom of slice; gradually pour cooled syrup over hot slice. Cool slice in tin.

sugar syrup Combine the water, juice and sugar in medium saucepan; bring to a boil. Simmer, uncovered, about 20 minutes or until syrup reduces to about 2½ cups. Cool to room temperature. Add orange flower water, cover; refrigerate 3 hours or overnight. (Syrup is best made the day before, covered and refrigerated; remove from refrigerator when slice goes into the oven so that syrup is at room temperature before pouring over hot slice.)

makes 28

Known variously throughout the Middle East and North Africa as basboosa, namoura or harisi, this sweet slice is saturated with a citrusy sugar syrup.

custard slice

¼ cup (40g) semolina
1½ cups (330g) caster sugar
¼ cup (35g) cornflour
6 eggs, beaten lightly
1 teaspoon grated lemon rind
1 litre (4 cups) milk
½ cup (80g) semolina, extra
12 sheets filo pastry
125g ghee, melted

syrup
1 medium lemon
1½ cups (330g) caster sugar
¾ cup (180ml) water
1 cinnamon stick

syrup Using a vegetable peeler, peel rind thinly from half the lemon. Combine sugar and water in saucepan; stir over heat, without boiling, until sugar is dissolved. Add rind and cinnamon; simmer, uncovered, without stirring, 2 minutes. Cool, discard rind and cinnamon.

1 Combine semolina, sugar, cornflour, eggs and rind in bowl; whisk until thick and combined. Bring milk to boil in pan; gradually whisk hot milk into egg mixture. Return mixture to pan.
2 Stir over heat until mixture begins to thicken, gradually add extra semolina; stir until thick, do not boil. Cool slightly.
3 Preheat oven to moderate. Lightly grease 22cm x 30cm ovenproof dish (2.5 litre/10 cup capacity).
4 To prevent pastry from drying out, cover with baking parchment then a damp tea towel until you are ready to use it. Brush a pastry sheet with ghee, place into prepared dish so that edges overhang sides. Repeat with five more pastry sheets and ghee, allowing pastry to overhang opposite sides of dish.
5 Pour custard mixture evenly into pastry case. Layer remaining sheets of pastry with ghee, place on top of custard, trim overlapping edges of pastry, fold ends inside dish to enclose filling. Brush with remaining ghee. Using sharp knife, score pastry diagonally, cutting though only one layer of pastry. Bake in moderate oven 45 minutes or until custard is set.
6 Meanwhile, make syrup. Pour cold syrup evenly over hot slice; cool in dish before cutting.

serves *8 to 10*

Filo is a dough native to the Middle East made from flour, water and a little oil. It is rolled into thin, almost translucent sheets and used in everything from main dishes to pastries and desserts.

drinks

spiced milk tea

1 star anise
2 cloves
1 cardamom pod
2 coriander seeds
1 teaspoon ground ginger
1 cinnamon stick, halved
2 jasmine tea bags
½ cup (110g) caster sugar
1 litre (4 cups) water
3 cups (750ml) milk
¼ cup (20g) flaked almonds, toasted, crushed

1 Using a mortar and pestle, lightly crush star anise, cloves, cardamom and coriander.
2 Combine anise mixture, ginger, cinnamon, tea bags, sugar, water and milk in large pan, stir over heat, without boiling, until sugar dissolves; bring to boil. Strain mixture into jug; serve warm topped with nuts.

makes about 1.75 litres (7 cups)

cardamom coffee

3 cardamom pods
2 tablespoons coarsely ground dark roasted coffee beans
1 teaspoon sugar
1 cup (250ml) water

1 Place cardamom pods on oven tray. Toast in moderate oven 4 minutes; cool. Using a mortar and pestle, lightly crush pods.
2 Combine cardamom, coffee, sugar and water in small pan, stir over heat until mixture comes up to boiling point; remove from heat.
3 Stand for 1 or 2 minutes to allow coffee grains to settle. Strain into tiny coffee cups and serve.

serves 4

almond milk

¼ cup (40g) blanched almonds, toasted
¾ cup (180ml) plain yogurt
2 cups (500ml) milk
½ teaspoon ground cinnamon
2 tablespoons caster sugar
6 ice cubes

1 Blend or process nuts until finely chopped.
2 Add remaining ingredients, blend or process until smooth.

makes *about 3 cups (750ml)*

iced mint tea

1½ cups firmly packed fresh mint leaves
3 Chinese green tea bags
2 tablespoons sugar
3 cups (750ml) boiling water

1 Combine mint, tea bags, sugar and water in large heatproof bowl, stand 15 minutes.
2 Strain mixture into jug; cool to room temperature. Refrigerate.

makes *about 3 cups (750ml)*

Mint tea, a traditional drink from the Middle East, is not only refreshing but is also good for the digestion. It can be served after a meal instead of coffee.

turkish delight

3 level tablespoons powdered gelatine
¼ cup (60ml) boiling water
3 cups (660g) caster sugar
2 cups (500ml) water, extra
¾ cup (110g) wheaten cornflour
2 tablespoons glucose syrup
50ml bottle rosewater essence
few drops red food colouring
1 cup (160g) icing sugar

1 Lightly oil a deep 19cm square cake tin; line base with baking parchment.
2 Sprinkle gelatine over boiling water in a small jug; stand jug in a small pan of simmering water. Stir until gelatine dissolves.
3 Combine the sugar with ¾ cup (180ml) of extra measured water in a medium saucepan; stir over a low heat until the sugar dissolves. Bring to boil; boil, without stirring, until temperature reaches 116°C (soft ball) on a sugar thermometer. Simmer at 116°C for 5 minutes, without stirring, regulating heat to maintain temperature at 116°C. Remove from heat.
4 Meanwhile, combine the remaining 1¼ cups (310ml) water and cornflour in a medium saucepan; whisk until smooth. Place over heat, bring to the boil, stirring constantly, until the mixture thickens.
5 Gradually whisk sugar syrup, gelatine mixture and glucose into cornflour mixture. Bring to the boil; reduce heat, simmer, stirring, for about 10 minutes or until the mixture thickens slightly. Remove from heat; stir in rosewater and add food colouring a drop at a time until the desired colour is achieved.
6 Strain mixture through fine sieve into prepared cake tin; skim any scum from surface. Stand for 15 minutes; cover surface with lightly oiled baking parchment. Stand at room temperature overnight.
7 Turn turkish delight onto a board dusted heavily with icing sugar; remove baking parchment. Cut into 36 squares, using a knife dipped in icing sugar between cuts. Roll squares in icing sugar. Store in an airtight container at room temperature, adding more icing sugar if needed.

makes *36 pieces*
tips *This recipe can be made a month ahead; keep well-coated in icing sugar and tightly sealed in an airtight container. To ensure success of recipe, use a sugar thermometer, available from kitchenware stores. For accurate measuring of gelatine, use a 20ml tablespoon.*

Turkish Delight is a soft,
jelly-like confection made
from starch and sugar.
It is often flavored with
rosewater, giving it a
characteristic pink colour.

turkish delight

conversion charts

measures

The cup and spoon measurements used in this book are metric: one measuring cup holds approximately 250ml; one metric tablespoon holds 20ml; one metric teaspoon holds 5ml.

All cup and spoon measurements are level. The most accurate way of measuring dry ingredients is to weigh them. When measuring liquids, use a clear glass or plastic jug with metric markings. We used large eggs with an average weight of 60g.

WARNING This book contains recipes for dishes made with raw or lightly cooked eggs. These should be avoided by vulnerable people such as pregnant and nursing mothers, invalids, the elderly, babies and young children.

dry measures

metric	imperial
15g	½oz
30g	1oz
60g	2oz
90g	3oz
125g	4oz (¼lb)
155g	5oz
185g	6oz
220g	7oz
250g	8oz (½lb)
280g	9oz
315g	10oz
345g	11oz
375g	12oz (¾lb)
410g	13oz
440g	14oz
470g	15oz
500g	16oz (1lb)
750g	24oz (1½lb)
1kg	32oz (2lb)

liquid measures

metric	imperial
30ml	1 fl oz
60ml	2 fl oz
100ml	3 fl oz
125ml	4 fl oz
150ml	5 fl oz (¼ pint/1 gill)
190ml	6 fl oz
250ml	8 fl oz
300ml	10 fl oz (½pt)
500ml	16 fl oz
600ml	20 fl oz (1 pint)
1000ml (1 litre)	1¾pints

length measures

metric	imperial
3mm	⅛in
6mm	¼in
1cm	½in
2cm	¾in
2.5cm	1in
5cm	2in
6cm	2½in
8cm	3in
10cm	4in
13cm	5in
15cm	6in
18cm	7in
20cm	8in
23cm	9in
25cm	10in
28cm	11in
30cm	12in (1ft)

oven temperatures

These oven temperatures are only a guide for conventional ovens. For fan-assisted ovens, check the manufacturer's manual.

	°C (Celcius)	°F (Fahrenheit)	gas mark
Very low	120	250	½
Low	150	275-300	1-2
Moderately low	170	325	3
Moderate	180	350-375	4-5
Moderately hot	200	400	6
Hot	220	425-450	7-8
Very hot	240	475	9

ACP BOOKS
General manager Christine Whiston
Test kitchen food director Pamela Clark
Editorial director Susan Tomnay
Creative director Hieu Chi Nguyen
Director of sales Brian Cearnes
Marketing manager Bridget Cody
Business analyst Rebecca Varela
Operations manager David Scotto
International rights enquiries Laura Bamford
lbamford@acpuk.com

acp books

ACP Books are published by ACP Magazines, a division of PBL Media Pty Limited
Group publisher, Women's lifestyle Pat Ingram
Director of sales, Women's lifestyle Lynette Phillips
Commercial manager, Women's lifestyle Seymour Cohen

Marketing director, Women's lifestyle Matthew Dominello
Public relations manager, Women's lifestyle Hannah Deveraux
Creative director, Events, Women's lifestyle Luke Bonnano
Research Director, Women's lifestyle Justin Stone
ACP Magazines, Chief Executive officer Scott Lorson
PBL Media, Chief Executive officer Ian Law

Produced by ACP Books, Sydney.
Published by ACP Books, a division of ACP Magazines Ltd, 54 Park St, Sydney; GPO Box 4088, Sydney, NSW 2001.
phone (02) 9282 8618 fax (02) 9267 9438.
acpbooks@acpmagazines.com.au
www.acpbooks.com.au
Printed and bound in China.

Australia Distributed by Network Services,
phone +61 2 9282 8777 fax +61 2 9264 3278
networkweb@networkservicescompany.com.au

United Kingdom Distributed by Australian Consolidated Press (UK),
phone (01604) 642 200 fax (01604) 642 300
books@acpuk.com
New Zealand Distributed by Netlink Distribution Company,
phone (9) 366 9966 ask@ndc.co.nz
South Africa Distributed by PSD Promotions,
phone (27 11) 392 6065/6/7
fax (27 11) 392 6079/80
orders@psdprom.co.za
Canada Distributed by Publishers Group Canada
phone (800) 663 5714 fax (800) 565 3770
service@raincoast.com

A catalogue record for this book is available from the British Library.
ISBN 978-1-903777-64-0
© ACP Magazines Ltd 2008
ABN 18 053 273 546
This publication is copyright. No part of it may be reproduced or transmitted in any form without the written permission of the publishers.